S0-BBU-430

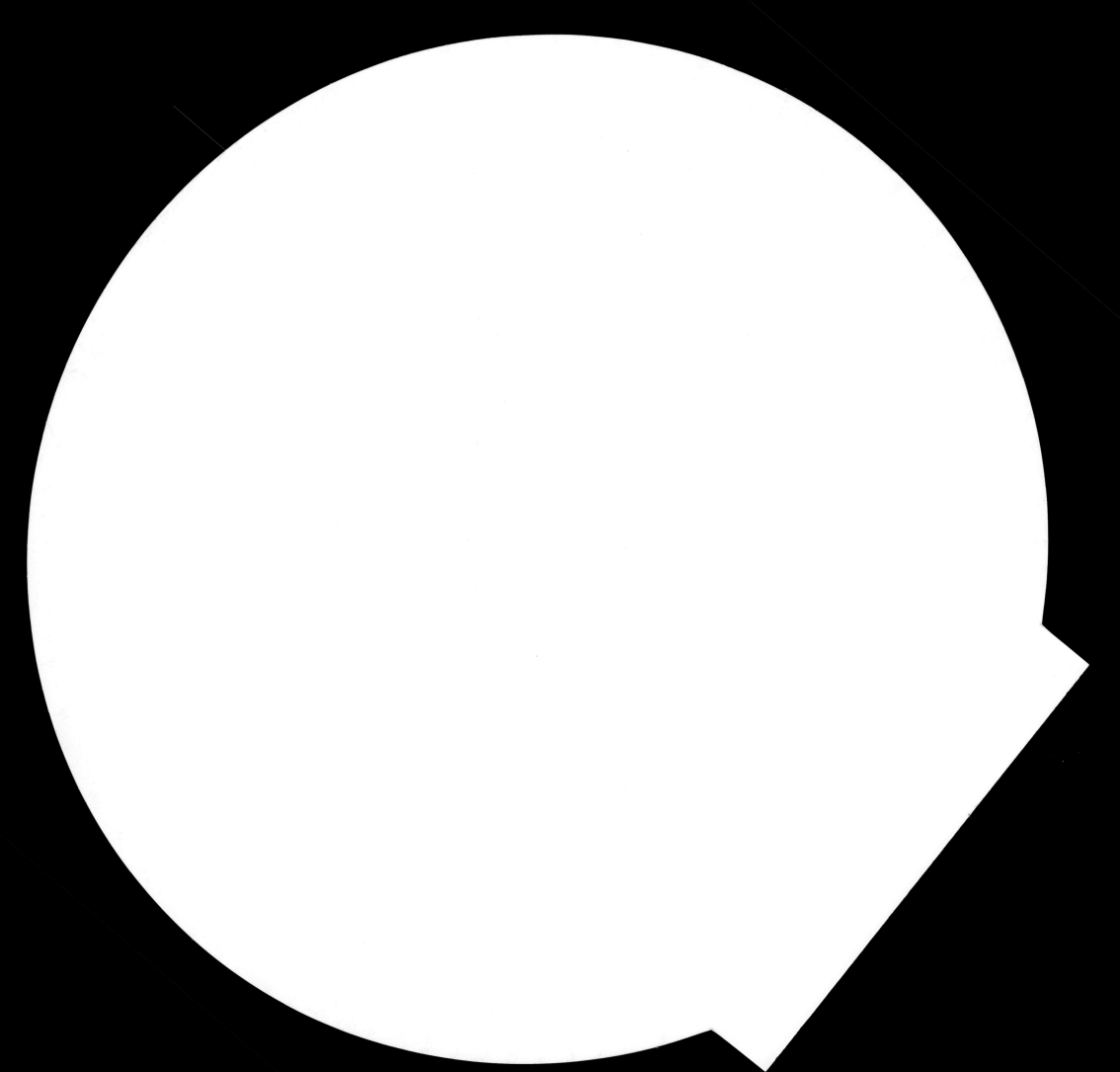

Pizza

How to Make and Bake More Than 50 Delicious Homemade Pizzas

Carla Bardi

Reader's
Digest

The Reader's Digest Association, Inc.
New York, NY

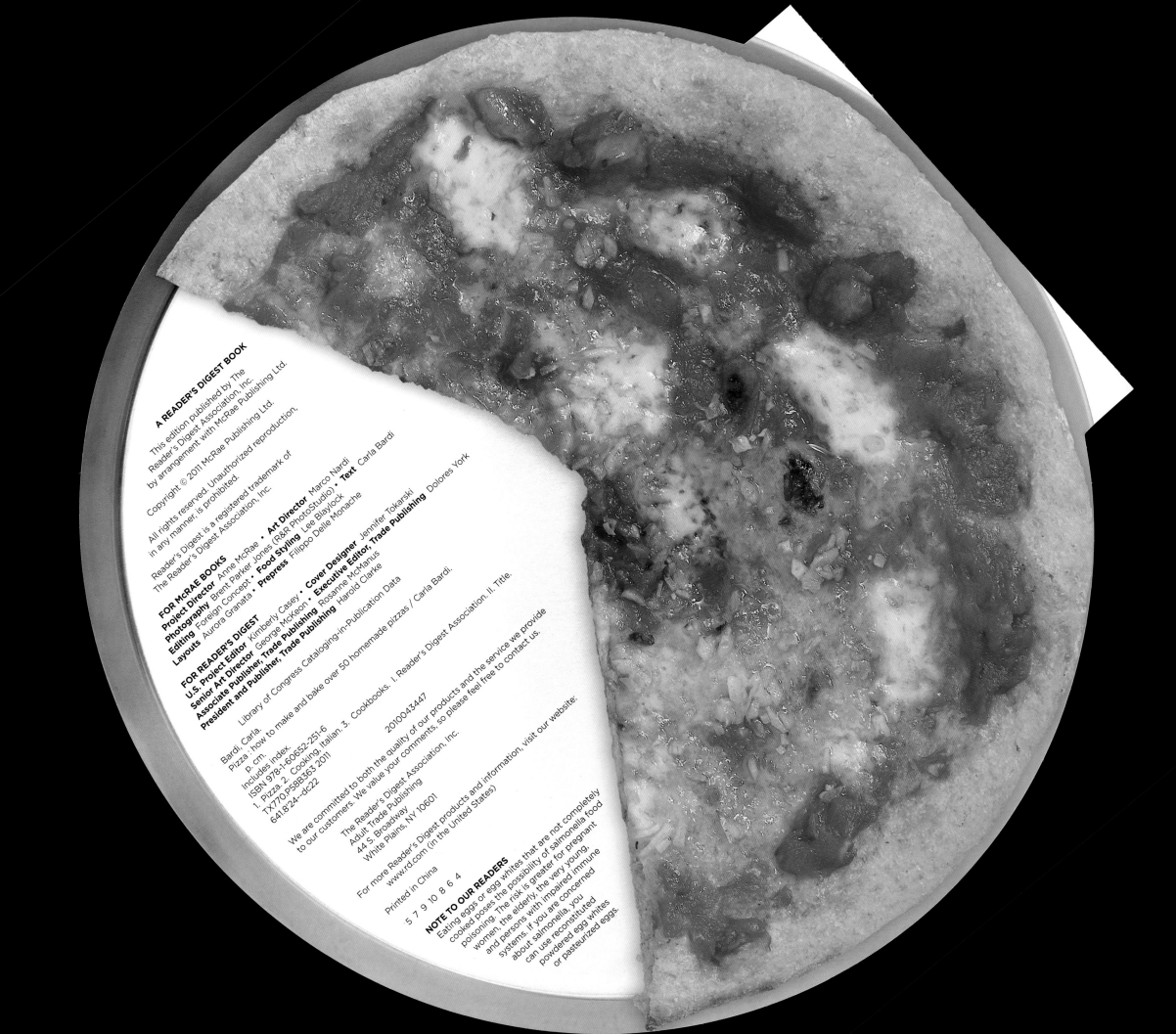

FOR McRAE BOOKS
Project Director Anne McRae • **Art Director** Marco Nardi
Photography Brent Parker Jones (R&R PhotoStudio) • **Text** Carla Bardi
Editing Foreign Concept • **Food Styling** Lee Blaylock
Layouts Aurora Granata • **Prepress** Filippo Delle Monache

FOR READER'S DIGEST
U.S. Project Editor Kimberly Casey • **Cover Designer** Jennifer Tokarski
Senior Art Director George McKeon • **Executive Editor, Trade Publishing** Dolores York
Associate Publisher, Trade Publishing Rosanne McManus
President and Publisher, Trade Publishing Harold Clarke

Library of Congress Cataloging-in-Publication Data

Bardi, Carla.
  Pizza : how to make and bake over 50 homemade pizzas / Carla Bardi.
       p. cm.
  Includes index.
  ISBN 978-1-60652-251-6
  1. Pizza. 2. Cooking, Italian. 3. Cookbooks. I. Reader's Digest Association. II. Title.
  TX770.P58B363 2011
  641.824--dc22
                                           2010043447

NOTE TO OUR READERS
Eating eggs or egg whites that are not completely
cooked poses the possibility of salmonella food
poisoning. The risk is greater for pregnant
women, the elderly, the very young,
and persons with impaired immune
systems. If you are concerned
about salmonella, you
can use reconstituted
powdered egg whites
or pasteurized eggs.

contents

truly international
Italian food

4

Of all things Italian, pizza—with its crisp, bready crust and classic tomato- and mozzarella-cheese topping—has truly conquered the world. The first pizza originated in the southern Italian city of Naples in the 18th and 19th centuries, where it was baked in wood ovens and then hawked in the narrow streets by boys from the bakeries, who announced their wares with piercing cries. Hungry customers chose slabs of pizza with various toppings to eat on the streets or to take home.

Over time, customers began to ask for more comfortable surroundings to enjoy their pizzas, and some enterprising bakers began offering seating, which is how the first pizzerias were born. These early pizzerias were very similar to what you will find all over Italy

today, and in many other parts of the world too: A room dominated by a vast wood-fired pizza oven and a marble bench with all the ingredients laid out and ready for use. Between the marble counter and the oven stand the skillful pizza-makers, whose often virtuoso performances include twirling sheets of dough on their fingertips and slapping them down hard on the cool marble benches. Some of these pizzerias became famous, and family dynasties of pizza-makers were born.

In 1889 Raffaele Esposito, the most well-known pizza-maker of the time, was invited to prepare the city's speciality for the king and queen of Italy who were visiting Naples. Esposito prepared three pizzas: the Mastunicola, topped with lard, cheese,

Opposite page: Pizzerias sprang up all over the United States. Lombardi's, founded in 1905 by Gennero Lombardi in Little Italy, Manhattan, was one of the first in New York.

and basil; the Marinara, topped with tomato, garlic, oil, and oregano; and one created especially for the occasion, made with tomato, oil, mozzarella cheese, and basil—ingredients that recall the red, white, and green of the Italian flag. The queen, whose name was Margherita, loved this last pizza and the proud pizzamaker named it in her honor. Her letter to Esposito, praising his culinary efforts on her behalf, is still proudly displayed in the Antica Pizzeria Brandi in Naples.

From its Neapolitan origins, pizza was exported all over the world by the droves of immigrants who left Italy in the 19th and early 20th centuries. Pizzerias sprang up in Italian neighborhoods in the United States, Canada, Argentina, Australia, and everywhere else the Italians

settled. But it wasn't until the second half of the 20th century that pizza really took off around the globe. Since then it has appeared almost everywhere, even to countries as far afield as Russia, Pakistan, and Brazil. As it has spread, pizza has taken on many of the flavors of traditional local cuisines. Many pizzas in France, for example, are topped with freshly grated Emmental cheese (delicious!), rather than traditional mozzarella, while in the United States regional styles, such as the hearty Chicago deep-dish pizza, have emerged.

As with all Italian food, there are few hard-and-fast rules beyond the use of the freshest and best ingredients. The traditional Italian arts of improvising and making do will also be of use. Divertitevi! (Have fun!)

Above: A modern-day pizza oven in Southern Italy.

making pizza
at home

There are many reasons why preparing pizza at home makes sense, even if there is a pizzeria or fast-food outlet with takeout pizza in your neighborhood. Making pizza is surprisingly easy and fun, and children will especially enjoy helping you to knead the dough and spread the toppings. Don't be put off by the idea of working with yeast for the crust: it really isn't difficult. And it isn't particularly time-consuming. You will need a few minutes to mix and knead the dough, but then it can be set aside to rise for an hour or two while you get on with other things. Most toppings are also quick and easy. Pizzerias and even take-out pizza is often expensive, while homemade pizza costs very little. The basic ingredients— flour, salt, yeast, tomato, and freshly grated cheese—are low-cost and readily available in supermarkets everywhere. Add a salad, and

you can prepare a hearty, nutritious, and mouthwatering meal for family and friends for next to nothing.

There are just one or two key things to remember for success every time. Bread flour will give the best results. In a pinch, you can use an unbleached, all-purpose (plain) flour, but the crust will be less crisp. We have shown you how to make the crust by hand, but it can also be whipped up in a food processor. You only need to pulse the ingredients for 30–45 seconds, until they come together. Home ovens cannot reach the same high temperatures as commercial ovens. For baking pizza we have suggested 10–15 minutes at 500°F (250°C/gas 10). Older ovens may not reach that temperature, and the pizza will take longer to cook. It doesn't matter; the crust will be slightly chewier, but still delicious and certainly less greasy than commercial pizza.

basic pizza dough

We have provided two recipes for the basic pizza crust. Those who enjoy a deep-dish type crust should use the thick one. Pizzas with hearty toppings will be better with the thicker crust. For best results, we suggest you use fresh or active dry yeast. You may also use instant or rapid-rise yeast, just remember that it doesn't need proofing.

MEDIUM CRUST

1/2 ounce (15 g) fresh yeast or 1 1/2 teaspoons active dry yeast

About 1 cup (250 ml) warm water

2 cups (300 g) bread flour + extra, to dust hands and work surface

1/3 teaspoon salt

1 tablespoon extra-virgin olive oil (optional)

SERVES 2 · PREPARATION 15-20 MINUTES
TIME TO RISE ABOUT 1 HOUR

THICK CRUST

3/4 ounce (25 g) fresh yeast or 2 teaspoons active dry yeast

About 1 1/3 cups (300 ml) warm water

3 cups (450 g) bread flour + extra, to dust hands and work surface

1/2 teaspoon salt

1 tablespoon extra-virgin olive oil (optional)

SERVES 2 · PREPARATION 15-20 MINUTES
TIME TO RISE ABOUT 1 HOUR

PREPARING THE YEAST

1. **Put** the fresh or active dry yeast in a small bowl and add about 1/2 cup (120 ml) of the warm water.

2. **Stir** gently until the yeast has dissolved. Set aside until frothy, about 10 minutes.

PREPARING THE DOUGH

1. Combine the flour and salt in a medium bowl. Pour in the yeast mixture, oil (if using), and enough of the remaining warm water to obtain a fairly sticky dough.

2. Dust a clean work surface with extra flour. Scrape all the dough out of the bowl onto the work surface. Shape into a firm, round ball.

3. Knead the dough for 8–10 minutes. When it is firm and no longer sticks to your hands or the work surface, lift it up and bang it down hard a couple of times to develop the gluten.

4. When ready, the dough will be smooth and elastic and show definite air bubbles beneath the surface. Place it in a large oiled bowl, and cover it with a cloth. Set aside to rise for 1 hour.

1. Don't worry about overworking or being too rough with the dough. Just make sure it doesn't become too dry and begin to crack.

2. Some people like a really thin crust. You can stretch the risen dough out to any thickness you like. Just make sure it doesn't break.

3. The heat in your hands helps develop the gluten (which is why we recommend kneading the dough by hand rather than in a food processor).

4. There is something deeply satisfying about kneading and handling pizza dough. Home-made pizza is both filling and fulfilling!

1. Place the dough in an oiled 12-inch (30-cm) pan and spread it with your fingertips, stretching it as you go, until it reaches the edges.

2. Press down around the edges of the pan to create a border, which will keep the topping from seeping off the pizza during cooking.

THE TOPPING

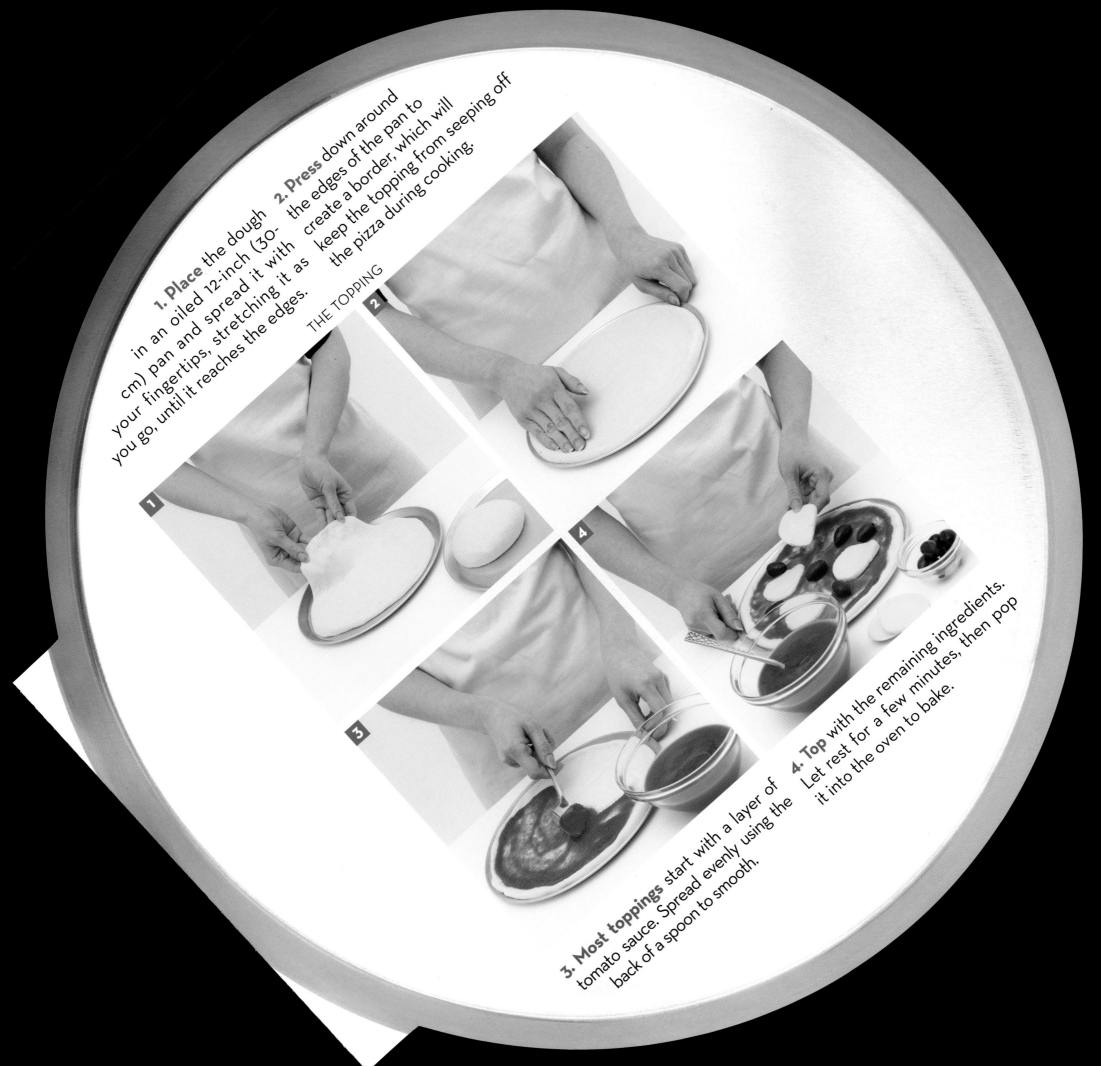

3. Most toppings start with a layer of tomato sauce. Spread evenly using the back of a spoon to smooth.

4. Top with the remaining ingredients. Let rest for a few minutes, then pop it into the oven to bake.

**1 ounce (30 g) fresh yeast or
2 teaspoons active dry yeast • About 1¹/₃ cups (300 ml)
lukewarm water • 1¹/₃ cups (200 g) whole-wheat (wholemeal) flour
• 1¹/₃ cups (200 g) bread flour • ¹/₂ teaspoon salt
• 1 tablespoon extra-virgin olive oil**

SERVES 2 • **PREPARATION** 15–20 MINUTES;
TIME TO RISE ABOUT 2 HOURS

whole-wheat (wholemeal)
pizza dough

1. Place the fresh or active dry yeast in a small bowl and add about ¹/₂ cup (120 ml) of the warm water. **2. Stir** gently until the yeast has dissolved. Set aside until frothy, about 10 minutes. **3. Combine** both flours and the salt in a medium bowl. Pour in the yeast mixture, oil, and enough of the remaining warm water to obtain a fairly sticky dough. Turn out onto a work surface lightly dusted with flour.

4. Knead the dough for 8–10 minutes. When it is firm and no longer sticks to your hands or the work surface, lift it up and bang it down hard a couple of times to develop the gluten. **5. When the dough** is ready, it will be smooth and elastic and show definite air bubbles beneath the surface. Place in a large oiled bowl and cover with a cloth. Set aside to rise until doubled in bulk, about 2 hours.

2½ teaspoons active dry yeast
· 1 teaspoon sugar · About 1 cup (250 ml) warm water
· 2 tablespoons extra-virgin olive oil · ½ teaspoon apple cider
vinegar · 1 tablespoon honey · ¼ cup (30 g) millet flour · 1 cup (150 g) white
rice flour · ¼ cup (30 g) arrowroot starch · ½ cup (75 g) tapioca flour · 2 teaspoons
xanthan gum · ¾ teaspoon salt · 1 large egg, at room temperature

SERVES 2 · PREPARATION 25-30 MINUTES
TIME TO RISE ABOUT 1 HOUR

gluten-free
pizza dough

1. Combine the yeast in a small bowl with the sugar and ½   dough hook, gradually adding enough of the remaining
cup (120 ml) of the warm water. Set aside until frothy,   water to obtain a stiff, shiny dough. **5. Shape** the dough
about 10 minutes. **2. Combine** the oil, apple cider vinegar,   into a ball and place in an oiled bowl. Cover with a clean
and honey in a small bowl. **3. Combine** the four types of   cloth or plastic wrap (cling film) and let rise until almost
flour, xanthan gum, and salt in a medium bowl. **4. Add** the   doubled in bulk, about 1 hour. **6. If you are gluten
yeast mixture, egg, and ⅓ cup (90 ml) of the remaining   intolerant,** use this crust for all the pizzas in this book.
warm water. Mix with an electric mixer using a paddle or

pizza margherita

CRUST

Basic pizza dough (see pages 8–11)

TOPPING

1 cup (250 g) diced canned tomatoes, with juice • Salt and freshly ground black pepper • 4 ounces (120 g) mozzarella cheese, thinly sliced or shredded 1 tablespoon extra-virgin olive oil (optional) • Fresh basil leaves, to garnish

SERVES 2 • PREPARATION 10 MINUTES + TIME TO PREPARE THE DOUGH & LET RISE

COOKING 10–15 MINUTES

CRUST **1. Prepare** the pizza dough following the instructions on pages 8–11. Set aside to rise. **2. Preheat** the oven to 500°F (250°C/gas 10). **3. Oil** a 12-inch (30-cm) pizza pan. **4. Knead** the risen pizza dough briefly on a lightly floured work surface, then press it into the prepared pan using your hands.

TOPPING **5. Spread** the tomatoes evenly over the dough, leaving a ½-inch (1-cm) border all around. Season with salt and pepper. Top with the mozzarella. **6. Bake** for 10–15 minutes, until the crust is crisp and golden brown and the mozzarella is bubbling and beginning to brown. **7. Drizzle** with the oil, if liked, and garnish with the basil. **8. Serve** hot.

This is a classic Italian pizza and many believe it was one of the first pizzas ever made. You can vary it by adding olives, capers, or garlic.

• If you liked this recipe, try the whole-wheat pizza with cheese, herbs & tomatoes on page 108.

pizza marinara

CRUST

Basic pizza dough (see pages 8–11)

TOPPING

1 cup (250 g) diced canned tomatoes, with juice
2 cloves garlic, thinly sliced · Salt · 1 teaspoon dried oregano
1 large ripe San Marzano or plum tomato, thinly sliced · 2 tablespoons extra-virgin olive oil
Fresh basil leaves, torn if large

SERVES 2 · **PREPARATION** 10 MINUTES + TIME TO PREPARE THE DOUGH & LET RISE

COOKING 10–15 MINUTES

CRUST 1. Prepare the pizza dough following the instructions on pages 8–11. Set aside to rise. **2. Preheat** the oven to 500°F (250°C/gas 10). **3. Oil** a 12-inch (30-cm) pizza pan. **4. Knead** the risen pizza dough briefly on a lightly floured work surface, then press it into the prepared pan using your hands.

TOPPING 5. Combine the canned tomatoes, garlic, salt, and oregano in a small bowl. Spread evenly over the dough, leaving a 1/2-inch (1-cm) border all around. Top with the sliced tomato. Drizzle with 1 tablespoon of oil. **5. Bake** for 10–15 minutes, until the crust is golden brown and crisp. **6. Drizzle** with the remaining 1 tablespoon of oil, and garnish with the basil. **7. Serve** hot.

San Marzano tomatoes come from the small town of San Marzano near Naples, in southern Italy. Long and pointy in shape, they have fewer seeds than most other tomatoes and a strong, sweet flavor.

● If you liked this recipe, try the pizza with cherry tomatoes & oregano on page 20.

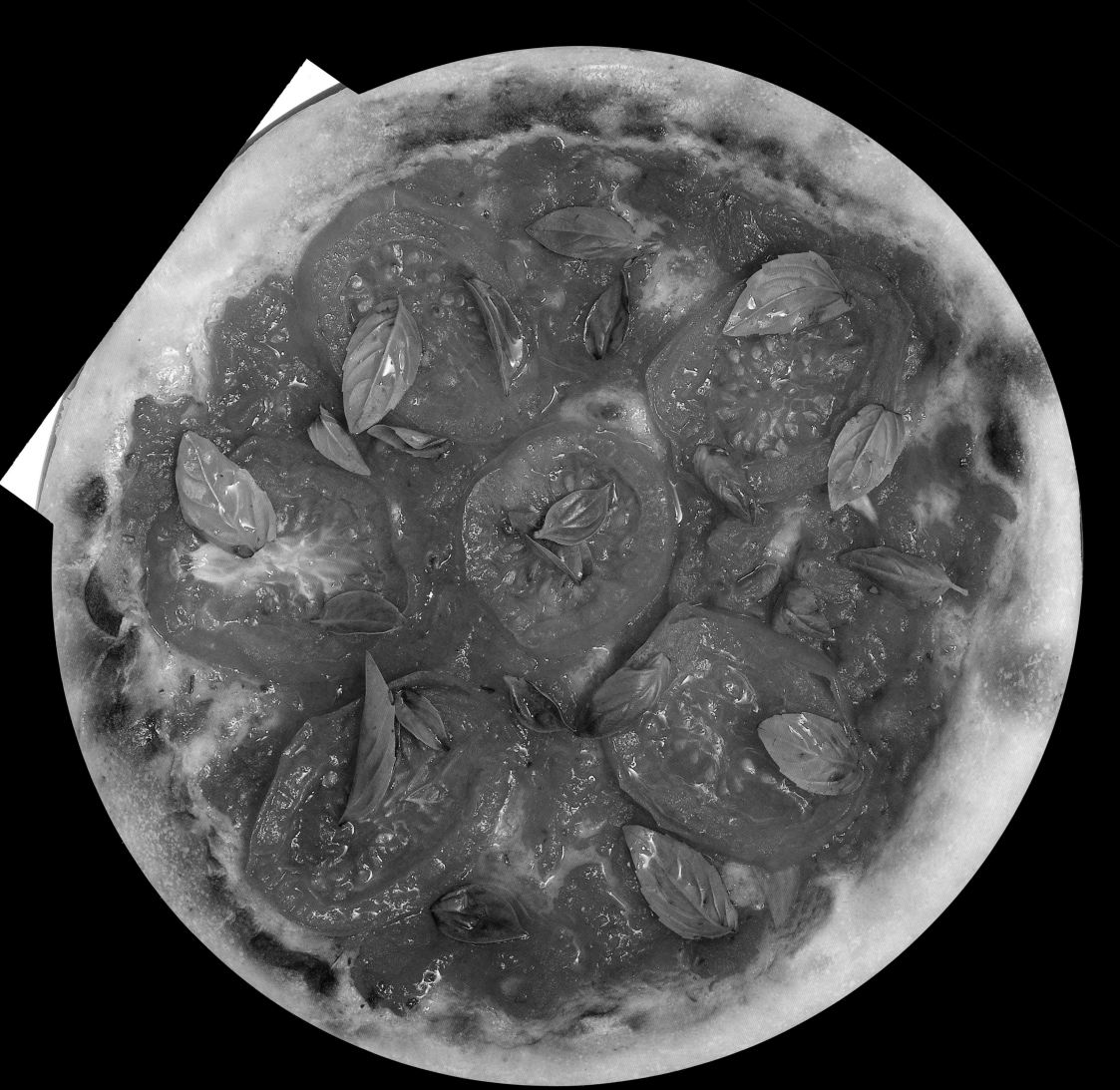

pizza **Napoletana**

CRUST

Basic pizza dough
(see pages 8–11)

TOPPING

1¹/₂ cups (350 g) diced canned tomatoes, with juice · 4 ounces (120 g) mozzarella cheese, thinly sliced or shredded · 10–12 salt-cured anchovy fillets · 1 tablespoon salt-cured capers, rinsed · ¹/₂ teaspoon dried oregano · 1 tablespoon extra-virgin olive oil

SERVES 2 · PREPARATION 15 MINUTES + TIME TO PREPARE THE DOUGH & LET RISE

COOKING 10–15 MINUTES

CRUST **1. Prepare** the pizza dough following the instructions on pages 8–11. Set aside to rise. **2. Preheat** the oven to 500°F (250°C/gas 10). **3. Oil** a 12-inch (30-cm) pizza pan. **4. Knead** the risen pizza dough briefly on a lightly floured work surface, then press it into the prepared pan using your hands. TOPPING **5. Spread** the tomatoes evenly over the dough, leaving a ¹/₂-inch (1-cm) border all around. Top with the mozzarella, anchovies, and capers. Sprinkle with the oregano. Drizzle with the oil. **6. Bake** for 10–15 minutes, until the crust is crisp and golden brown and the mozzarella is bubbling and beginning to brown. **7. Serve** hot.

In Italy, this pizza is made with fresh mozzarella made from water buffalo's milk (instead of the usual pasteurized cow's milk). A small amount of water buffalo mozzarella is now made in North America, and it is also imported from Italy. Try it, if you get the chance.

• If you liked this recipe, try the pissaladiere on page 112.

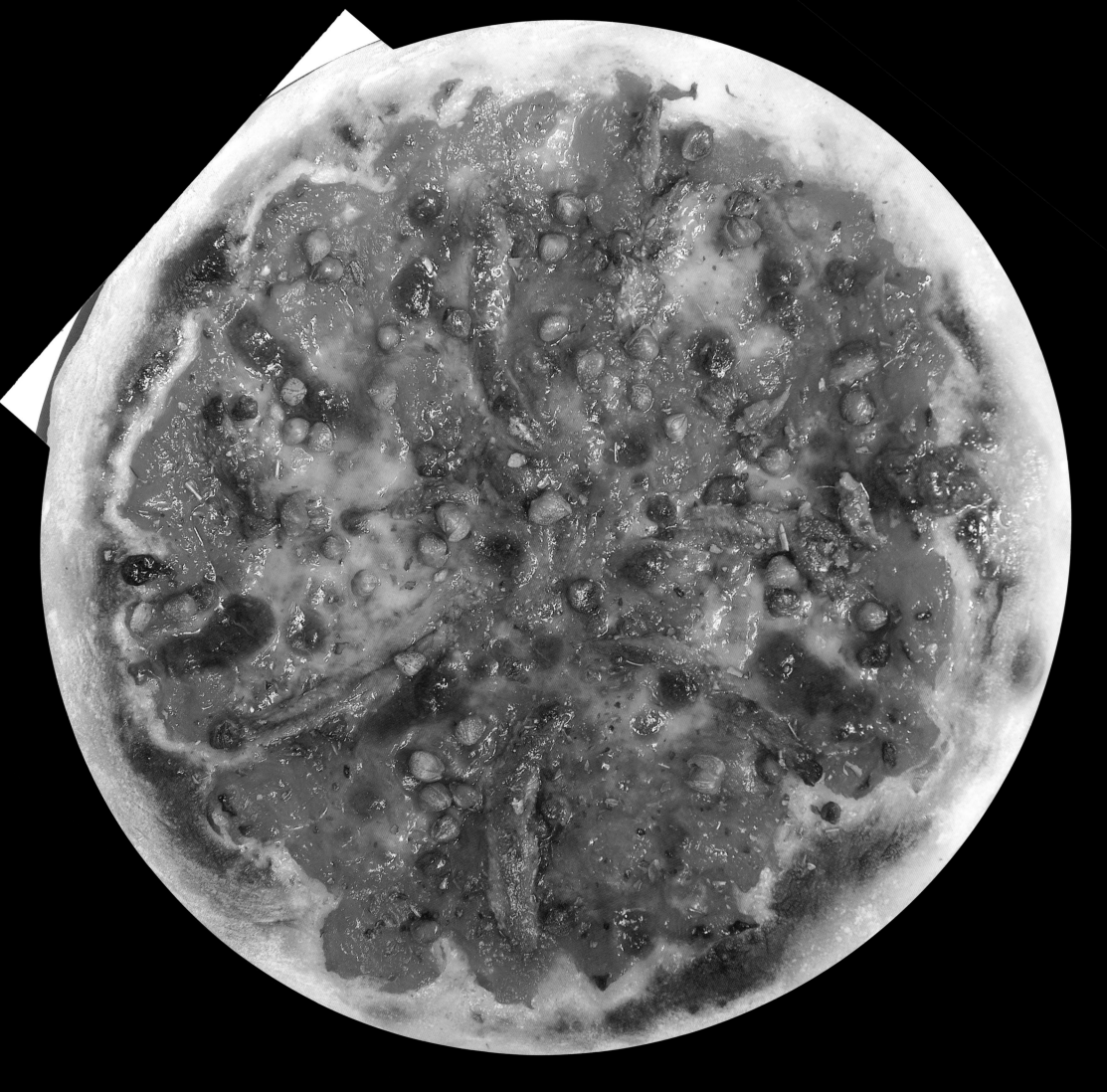

pizza with cherry tomatoes & oregano

CRUST

Basic pizza dough (see pages 8–11)

1 large potato, boiled and mashed · 1 tablespoon extra-virgin olive oil

TOPPING

12–16 cherry tomatoes, thinly sliced · Salt and freshly ground black pepper

1 teaspoon dried oregano · 2 tablespoons extra-virgin olive oil

SERVES 2 · PREPARATION 15 MINUTES + TIME TO BOIL THE POTATO, PREPARE THE DOUGH & LET RISE

COOKING 10–15 MINUTES

CRUST **1. Prepare** the pizza dough following the instructions on pages 8–11, incorporating the mashed potato and oil into it as you knead. Set aside to rise. **2. Preheat** the oven to 500°F (250°C/gas 10). **3. Oil** a 12-inch (30-cm) pizza pan. **4. Knead** the risen pizza dough briefly on a lightly floured work surface, then press it into the prepared pan using your hands. TOPPING **5. Place** the tomatoes on the dough, leaving a ½-inch (1-cm) border all around. Season with salt, pepper, and oregano. Drizzle with the oil. **6. Bake** for 10–15 minutes, until the crust is crisp and golden brown. **7. Serve** hot.

For a heartier dish, top the cherry tomatoes with a little mozzarella or freshly grated Emmental cheese.

• If you liked this recipe, try the pizza with cherry tomatoes & zucchini flowers on page 32.

whole-wheat pizza with **garlic**

CRUST

Whole-wheat (wholemeal) pizza dough (see page 12)

TOPPING

1 cup (250 g) diced canned tomatoes, with juice · 2-3 cloves garlic, finely sliced
4 ounces (120 g) mozzarella cheese, thinly sliced or shredded
1 tablespoon extra-virgin olive oil · Salt and freshly ground black pepper

SERVES 2 · **PREPARATION** 15 MINUTES + TIME TO PREPARE THE DOUGH & LET RISE
COOKING 10-15 MINUTES

CRUST 1. Prepare the whole-wheat pizza dough following the instructions on page 12. Set aside to rise for 2 hours. **2. Oil** a 12-inch (30-cm) pizza pan. **3. Knead** the risen pizza dough briefly on a lightly floured work surface, then press it into the prepared pan using your hands. Let rise for 30 minutes. **4. Preheat** the oven to 500°F (250°C/gas 10).

TOPPING 5. Spread the dough evenly with the tomatoes, leaving a ½-inch (1-cm) border all around. Sprinkle with the garlic and top with the mozzarella. Drizzle with the oil and season with salt and pepper. **6. Bake** for 10-15 minutes, until the crust is crisp and golden brown and the cheese is bubbling and beginning to brown. **7. Serve** hot.

The nutty flavor of the whole-wheat (wholemeal) crust melds beautifully with the strong garlic-flavored topping. Use more or less garlic, as you prefer.

● If you liked this recipe, try the whole-wheat pizza with vegetable topping on page 96.

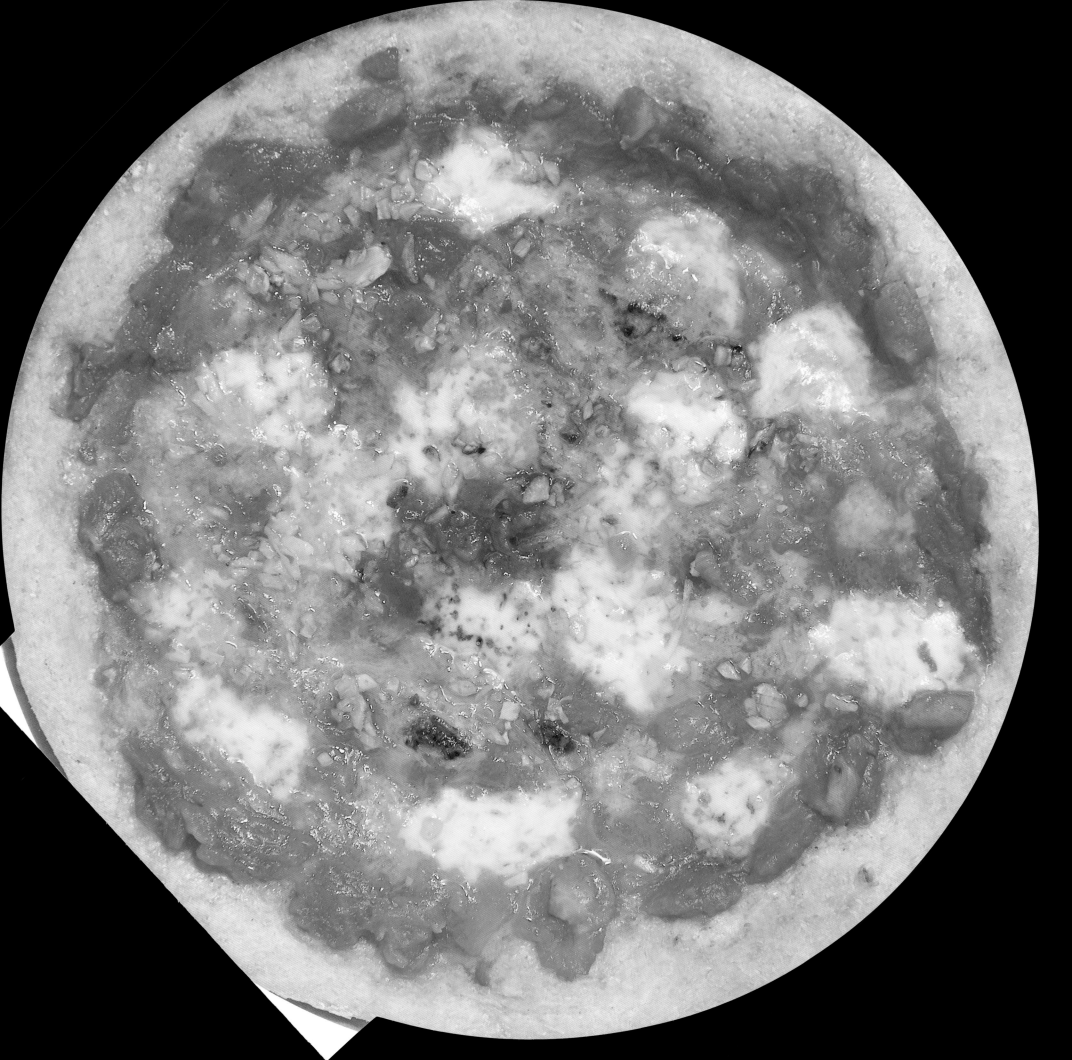

pizza with **onion & pesto**

CRUST
Basic pizza dough (see pages 8–11)

PESTO
1 large bunch basil • 2 cloves garlic • Salt • 2 tablespoons pine nuts
4 tablespoons freshly grated Parmesan cheese
1/2 cup (120 ml) extra-virgin olive oil

TOPPING
1 cup (250 g) diced canned tomatoes, with juice • Salt • 1–2 small white onions, finely sliced

SERVES 2 • PREPARATION 25 MINUTES + TIME TO PREPARE THE DOUGH & LET RISE
COOKING 10–15 MINUTES

CRUST **1. Prepare** the pizza dough following the instructions on pages 8–11. Set aside to rise. **2. Preheat** the oven to 500°F (250°C/gas 10). **3. Oil** a 12-inch (30-cm) pizza pan.

PESTO **4. Pesto** Chop the basil and garlic with a pinch of salt in a food processor. Add the pine nuts and Parmesan and chop until smooth. Stir in the oil. The pesto should be smooth and dense.

TOPPING **5. Knead** the risen pizza dough briefly on a lightly floured work surface, then press it into the prepared pan using your hands. **6. Spread** the tomatoes evenly over the dough, leaving a 1/2-inch (1-cm) border all around. Top with the onions and season with salt. **7. Bake** for 10–15 minutes, until the crust is crisp and golden brown and the onions are tender and cooked. **8. Dot** with the pesto. **9. Serve** hot.

This recipe will make almost 1 cup (250 ml) of pesto, which is enough for two pizzas. If you are only making one pizza, the remaining pesto can be stored in the refrigerator for 2–3 days. Serve it on pasta or smear it over freshly baked bread or focaccia.

• If you liked this recipe, try the pizza with 4 cheeses & pesto on page 102.

24

cheese pizza
with **onion, apple & walnuts**

CRUST

Basic pizza dough (see pages 8–11)

TOPPING

¹/₄ cup (60 g) butter · 2 small white onions, sliced · 2 cloves garlic, thinly sliced · ¹/₄ cup (60 ml) brandy · ¹/₄ cup (60 ml) heavy (double) cream · Freshly squeezed juice of ¹/₂ lemon · 3 ounces (90 g) mozzarella cheese, thinly sliced or shredded · 6–8 walnuts, halved

SERVES 2 · PREPARATION 30 MINUTES + TIME TO PREPARE THE DOUGH & LET RISE
COOKING 20–25 MINUTES

CRUST **1. Prepare** the pizza dough following the instructions on pages 8–11. Set aside to rise. **2. Preheat** the oven to 500°F (250°C/gas 10). **3. Oil** a 12-inch (30-cm) pizza pan. **TOPPING** **4. Melt** the butter in a large frying pan over medium heat. Add the onions and garlic and sauté until softened, 3–4 minutes. **5. Add** the brandy and sauté until evaporated, 2–3 minutes. Stir in the cream and simmer for 2 minutes. Season with salt and pepper and remove from the heat. **6. Thinly slice** the apples and brush with the lemon juice. **7. Knead** the risen pizza dough briefly on a lightly floured work surface, then press it into the prepared pan using your hands. **8. Spread** the onion mixture over the dough, leaving a ¹/₂-inch (1-cm) border all around. Top with the Fontina, mozzarella, and apples. Season with salt and top with the walnuts. **9. Bake** for 10–15 minutes, until the crust is crisp and golden brown and the cheeses are bubbling and beginning to brown. **10. Serve** hot.

This is a hearty topping; be sure to use the thicker dough (see page 8.) Choose a crisp, tangy apple for the topping; Granny Smiths are ideal.

• **If you liked this recipe, try the pizza with onion, cheese & walnuts on page 114.**

26

pizza with Gorgonzola & pineapple

CRUST

Basic pizza dough (see pages 8-11)

TOPPING

4 ounces (100 g) mozzarella cheese, thinly sliced or shredded
4 ounces (100 g) Gorgonzola cheese, cut into small cubes • 1 clove garlic,
thinly sliced • 3/4 cup (120 g) canned pineapple pieces, drained
1 tablespoon extra-virgin olive oil • Cracked pepper

SERVES 2 • PREPARATION 15 MINUTES + TIME TO PREPARE THE DOUGH & LET RISE
COOKING 10-15 MINUTES

CRUST **1. Prepare** the pizza dough following the instructions on pages 8-11. Set aside to rise. **2. Preheat** the oven to 500°F (250°C/gas 10). **3. Oil** a 12-inch (30-cm) pizza pan. **4. Knead** the risen pizza dough briefly on a lightly floured work surface, then press it into the prepared pan using your hands.
TOPPING **5. Spread** the dough with the mozzarella, Gorgonzola, garlic, and pineapple, leaving a 1/2-inch (1-cm) border all around. Drizzle with oil and season with cracked pepper. **6. Bake** for 10-15 minutes, until the crust is crisp and golden brown and the cheeses are bubbling and beginning to brown. **7. Serve** hot.

If preferred, use fresh pineapple in the topping. Choose a small, sweet pineapple, peel and remove the hard core, and cut into small pieces.

● If you liked this recipe, try the gluten-free pizza on page 110.

28

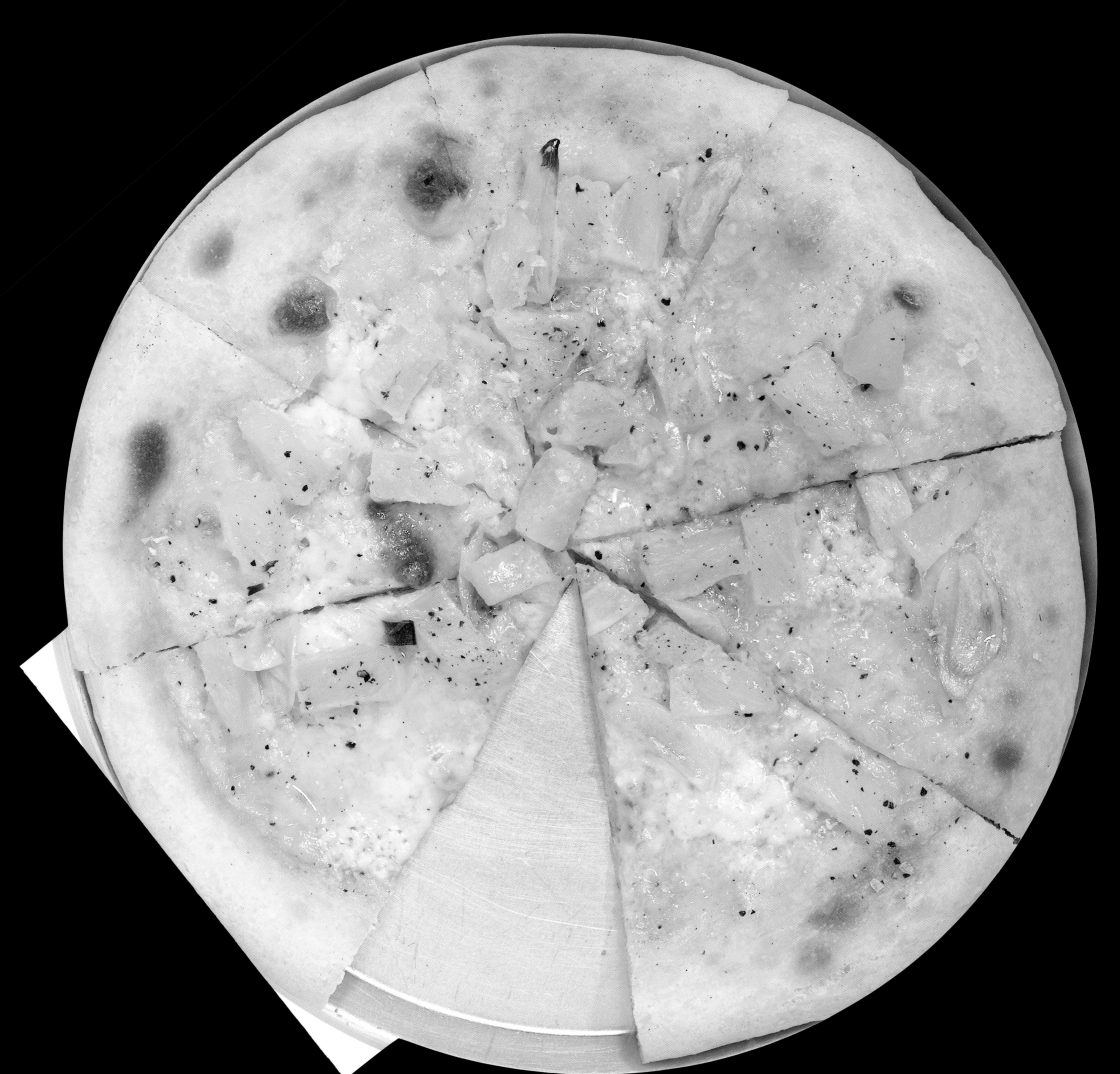

pizza bianca

CRUST

Basic pizza dough (see pages 8–11)

TOPPING

1 tablespoon salt pork, chopped · 1 cup (120 g) freshly grated Parmesan cheese · Cracked pepper · Fresh basil leaves, torn if large, to garnish

SERVES 2 · **PREPARATION** 15 MINUTES + TIME TO PREPARE THE DOUGH & LET RISE

COOKING 10–15 MINUTES

CRUST 1. Prepare the pizza dough following the instructions on pages 8–11. Set aside to rise. **2. Preheat** the oven to 500°F (250°C/gas 10). **3. Oil** a 12-inch (30-cm) pizza pan. **4. Knead** the risen pizza dough briefly on a lightly floured work surface, then press it into the prepared pan using your hands.

TOPPING 5. Sprinkle with the salt pork, cover with the cheese, and season with cracked pepper. **6. Bake** for 10–15 minutes, until the crust is crisp and golden brown and the cheese is bubbling and beginning to brown. **7. Garnish** with the basil. **8. Serve** hot.

This simple pizza makes a wonderful snack or appetizer.

● **If you liked this recipe, try the pizza with garlic, arugula & Parmesan on page 36.**

30

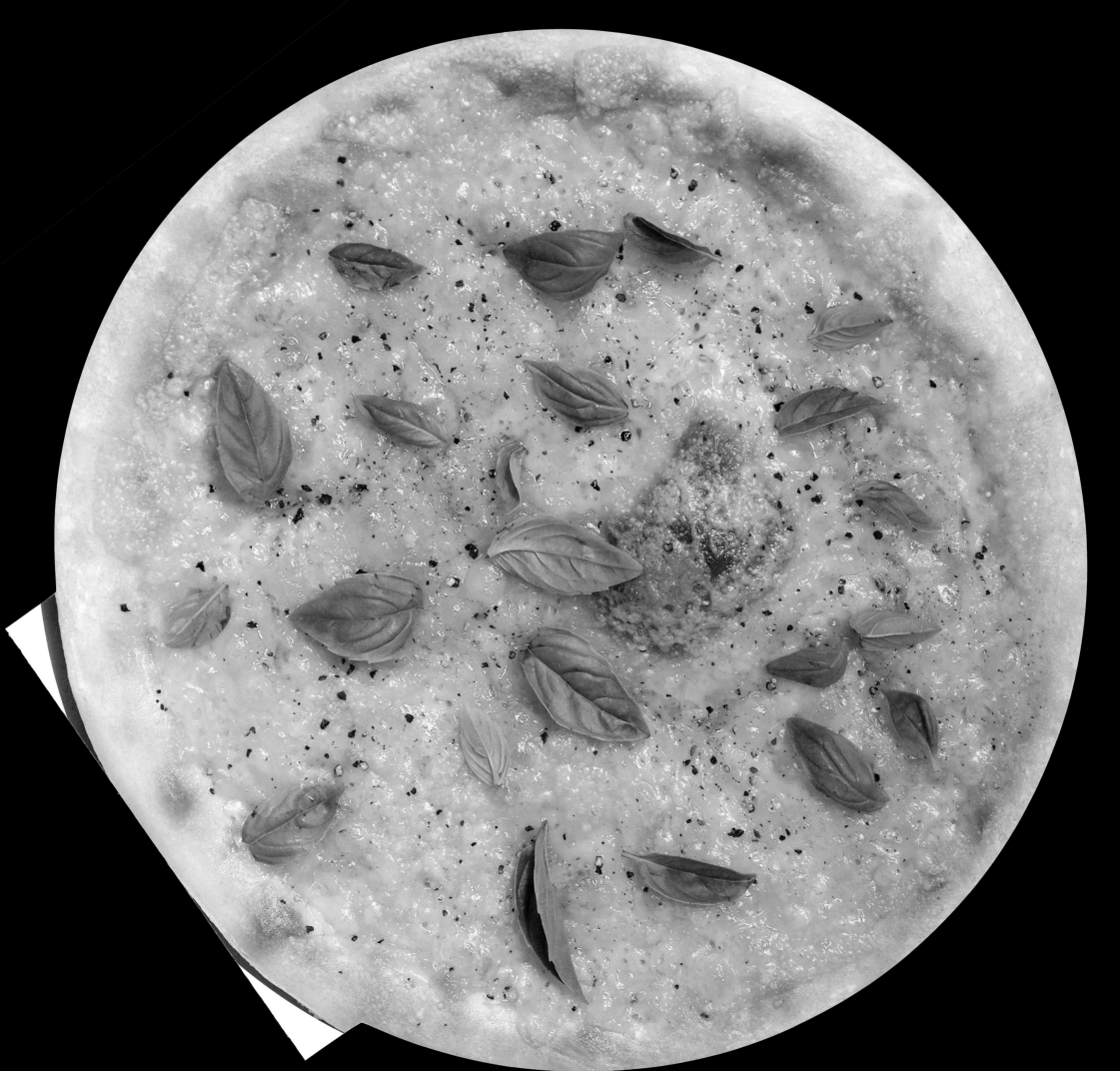

pizza with cherry tomatoes & zucchini flowers

CRUST

Basic pizza dough (see pages 8–11)

TOPPING

2 tablespoons extra-virgin olive oil • 5 ounces (150 g) fresh mozzarella cheese, thinly sliced • 4–6 large zucchini (courgette) flowers, rinsed and dried 6–8 cherry tomatoes, halved • Salt and freshly ground black or white pepper

SERVES 2 • PREPARATION 15 MINUTES + TIME TO PREPARE THE DOUGH & LET RISE

COOKING 10–15 MINUTES

CRUST 1. **Prepare** the pizza dough following the instructions on pages 8–11. Set aside to rise. 2. **Preheat** the oven to 500°F (250°C/gas 10). 3. **Oil** a 12-inch (30-cm) pizza pan. 4. **Knead** the risen pizza dough briefly on a lightly floured work surface, then press it into the prepared pan using your hands. TOPPING 5. **Drizzle** the dough with 1 tablespoon of oil and cover with the mozzarella, leaving a ½-inch (1-cm) border all around. Top with the zucchini flowers and cherry tomatoes and drizzle with the remaining oil. Season with salt and pepper. 6. **Bake** for 10–15 minutes, until the base is crisp and golden brown and the cheese is bubbling and beginning to brown. 7. **Serve** hot.

Zucchini flowers are available in farmer's markets in spring and summer. Their fresh, delicate taste adds a touch of class to this pizza. Serve it with a glass of cool, crisp white wine.

● If you liked this recipe, try the pizza capricciosa on page 40.

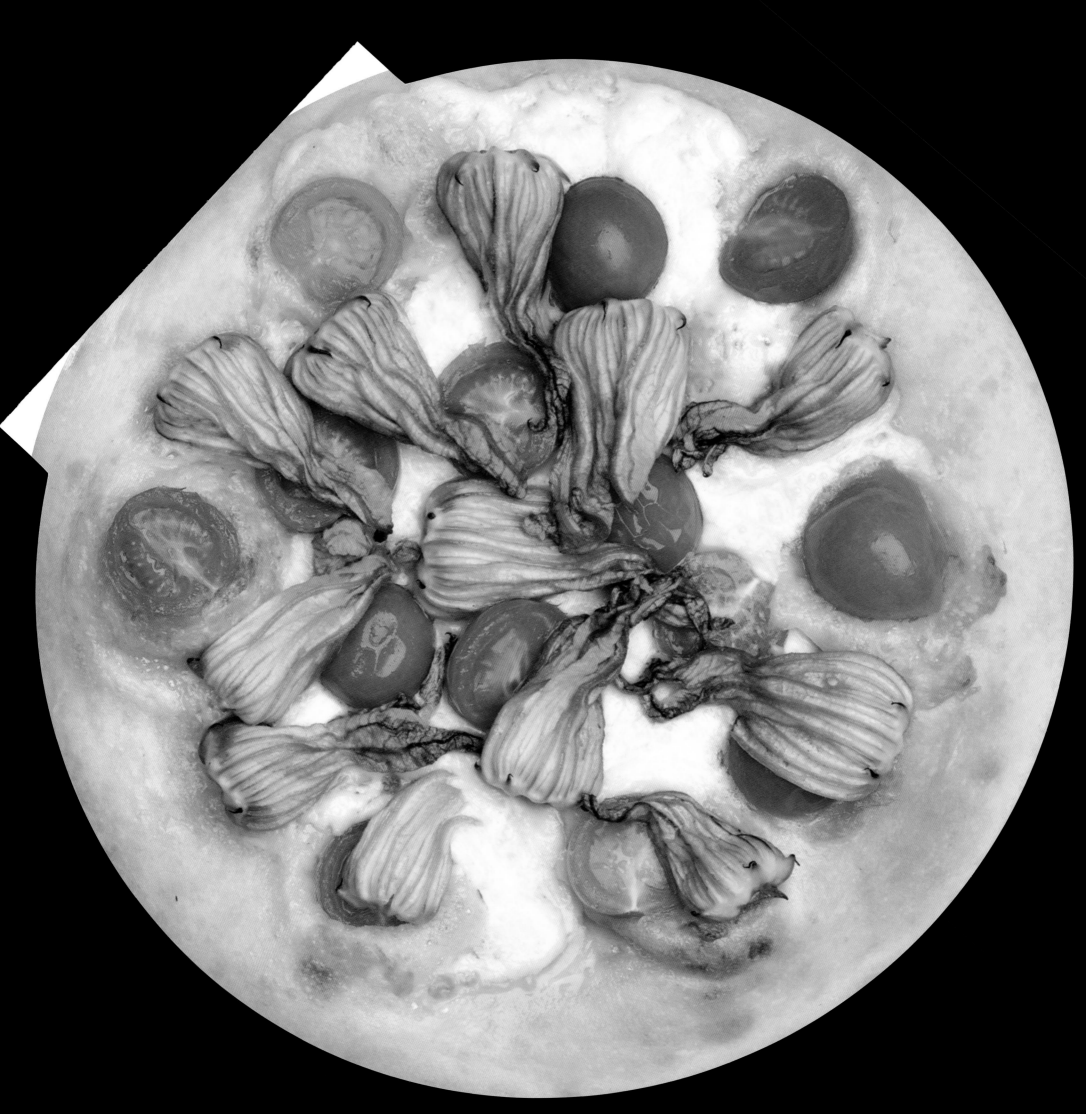

pizza with **garlic & arugula**

CRUST

Basic pizza dough (see pages 8–11)

TOPPING

3–4 cloves garlic, thinly sliced • 4–6 tablespoons freshly grated Parmesan cheese • 2 tablespoons extra-virgin olive oil • 1 small bunch baby arugula (rocket) • Salt and freshly ground black pepper

SERVES 2 • **PREPARATION** 10 MINUTES + TIME TO PREPARE THE DOUGH & LET RISE

COOKING 10–15 MINUTES

CRUST 1. Prepare the pizza dough following the instructions on pages 8–11. Set aside to rise. **2. Preheat** the oven to 500°F (250°C/gas 10). **3. Oil** a 12-inch (30-cm) pizza pan. **4. Knead** the risen pizza dough briefly on a lightly floured work surface, then press it into the prepared pan using your hands.

TOPPING 5. Sprinkle the dough with the garlic and Parmesan, leaving a ½-inch (1-cm) border all around. Drizzle with 1 tablespoon of oil. **6. Bake** for 10–15 minutes, until the crust is crisp and golden brown. **7. Top** with the arugula and drizzle with the remaining 1 tablespoon of oil. **8. Season** with salt and pepper. **9. Serve** hot.

Another simple, flavorful pizza. Be sure to use only the best quality, cold-pressed extra-virgin olive oil.

● If you liked this recipe, try the pizza with apple & Gorgonzola on page 76.

garlic, arugula & Parmesan

pizza with

CRUST

Basic pizza dough (see pages 8–11)

TOPPING

1 cup (250 g) diced canned tomatoes, with juice · 3 cloves garlic, thinly sliced
2 ounces (60 g) mozzarella cheese, thinly sliced or shredded · Salt
1 large black olive · Fresh basil leaves, torn if large · Small bunch baby arugula (rocket) leaves
2 ounces (60 g) Parmesan cheese, shaved · Cracked pepper

SERVES 2 · PREPARATION 15 MINUTES + TIME TO PREPARE THE DOUGH & LET RISE
COOKING 10–15 MINUTES

CRUST **1. Prepare** the pizza dough following the instructions on pages 8–11. Set aside to rise. **2. Preheat** the oven to 500°F (250°C/gas 10). **3. Oil** a 12-inch (30-cm) pizza pan. **4. Knead** the risen pizza dough briefly on a lightly floured work surface, then press it into the prepared pan using your hands.

TOPPING **5. Spread** the tomatoes evenly over the dough, leaving a ½-inch (1-cm) border all around. Top with the garlic and mozzarella. Season with salt. Place the olive in the center. **6. Bake** for 10–15 minutes, until the crust is crisp and golden brown and the cheese is bubbling and beginning to brown. **7. Top** with the basil, arugula, and Parmesan. Season with cracked pepper. **8. Serve** hot.

You can replace the Parmesan with another aged, highly flavored cheese, such as pecorino or ricotta salata,

● If you liked this recipe, try the pizza with garlic & arugula on page 34.

ham pizza

CRUST

Basic pizza dough (see pages 8–11)

TOPPING

2 tablespoons extra-virgin olive oil · 3 ounces (90 g) ham, thinly sliced, each slice torn in 2-3 pieces · 4 ounces (120 g) mozzarella cheese, thinly sliced or shredded · Freshly ground black pepper or ½ teaspoon crushed red pepper flakes (optional)

SERVES 2 · PREPARATION 15 MINUTES + TIME TO PREPARE THE DOUGH & LET RISE

COOKING 10–15 MINUTES

CRUST **1. Prepare** the pizza dough following the instructions on pages 8–11. Set aside to rise. **2. Preheat** the oven to 500°F (250°C/gas 10). **3. Oil** a 12-inch (30-cm) pizza pan. **4. Knead** the risen pizza dough briefly on a lightly floured work surface, then press it into the prepared pan using your hands.

TOPPING **5. Brush** the dough with a little oil and arrange the ham on top, leaving a ½-inch (1-cm) border all around. Sprinkle with the mozzarella and pepper, if desired. **6. Bake** for 10–15 minutes, until the crust is crisp and golden brown and the cheese is bubbling and just beginning to brown. **7. Drizzle** with the remaining oil. **8. Serve** hot.

For a slightly different flavor, replace the ham with the same quantity of prosciutto (Parma ham);

● **If you liked this recipe, try the white pizza with prosciutto & arugula on page 64.**

38

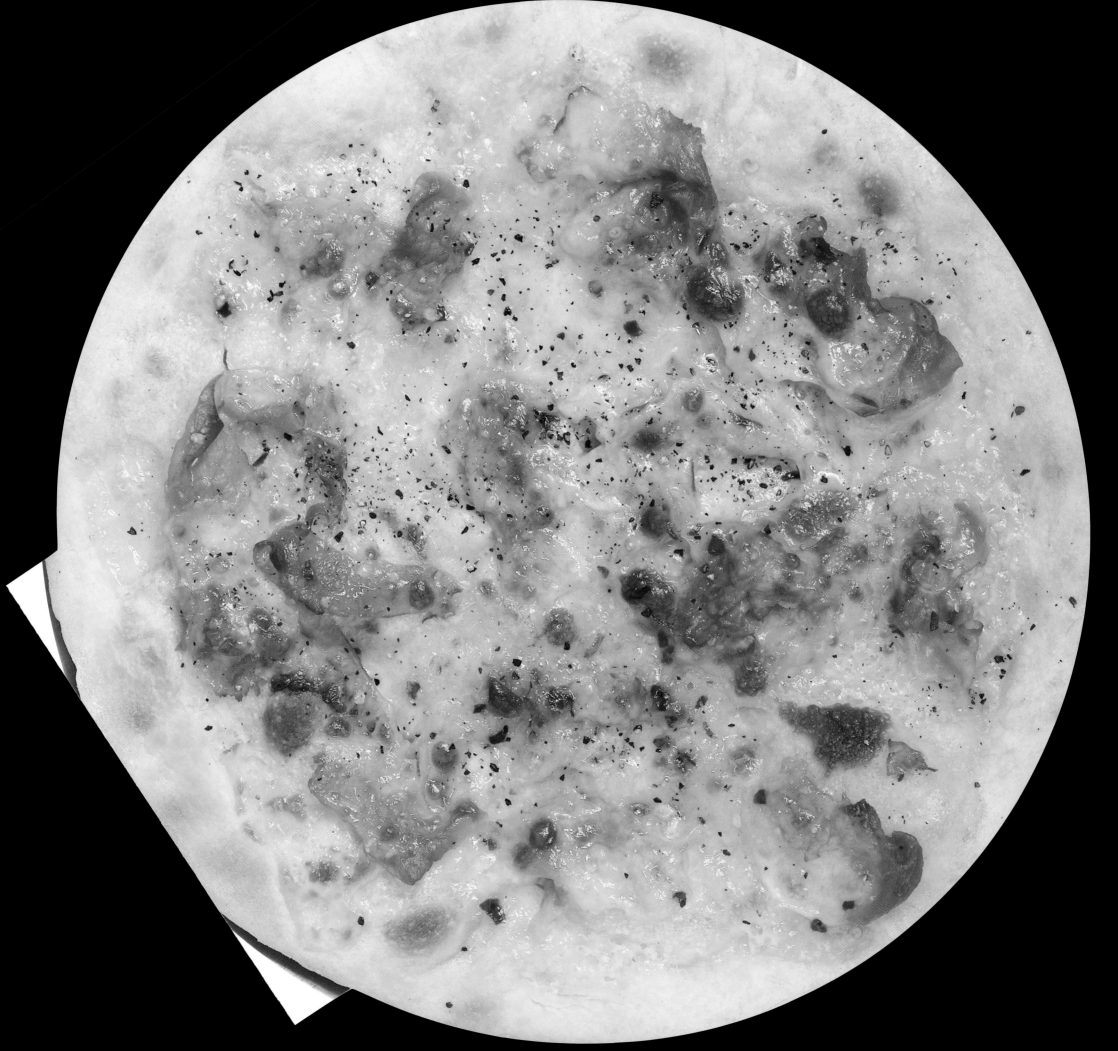

CRUST

Basic pizza dough (see pages 8–11)

TOPPING

1 cup (250 g) diced canned tomatoes, with juice • 2 ounces (60 g) ham, cut in strips • 6 salt-cured anchovy fillets, crumbled • 4 ounces (120 g) mozzarella cheese, thinly sliced or shredded • 2 artichoke hearts preserved in oil, drained, and halved 3–4 button mushrooms, halved • 3–4 green olives, pitted and thinly sliced • 1 clove garlic, thinly sliced • ½ teaspoon dried oregano • 1 tablespoon extra-virgin olive oil

SERVES 2 • **PREPARATION** 25 MINUTES + TIME TO PREPARE THE DOUGH & LET RISE
COOKING 10–15 MINUTES

pizza capricciosa

CRUST **1. Prepare** the pizza dough following the instructions on pages 8–11. Set aside to rise. **2. Preheat** the oven to 500°F (250°C/gas 10). **3. Oil** a 12-inch (30-cm) pizza pan. **4. Knead** the risen pizza dough briefly on a lightly floured work surface, then press it into the prepared pan using your hands. TOPPING **5. Spread** the tomatoes evenly over the dough, leaving a ½-inch (1-cm) border all around. Top with the ham, anchovies, mozzarella, artichokes, mushrooms, olives, and garlic. Sprinkle with the oregano and drizzle with the oil. **6. Bake** for 10–15 minutes, until the crust is crisp and golden brown and the cheese is bubbling and beginning to brown. **7. Serve** hot.

Capricciosa is "whimsical" in Italian and means that there are no precise ingredients for the topping; choose whatever you like. These are the most commonly used ingredients.

● **If you liked this recipe, try the four seasons pizza on page 44.**

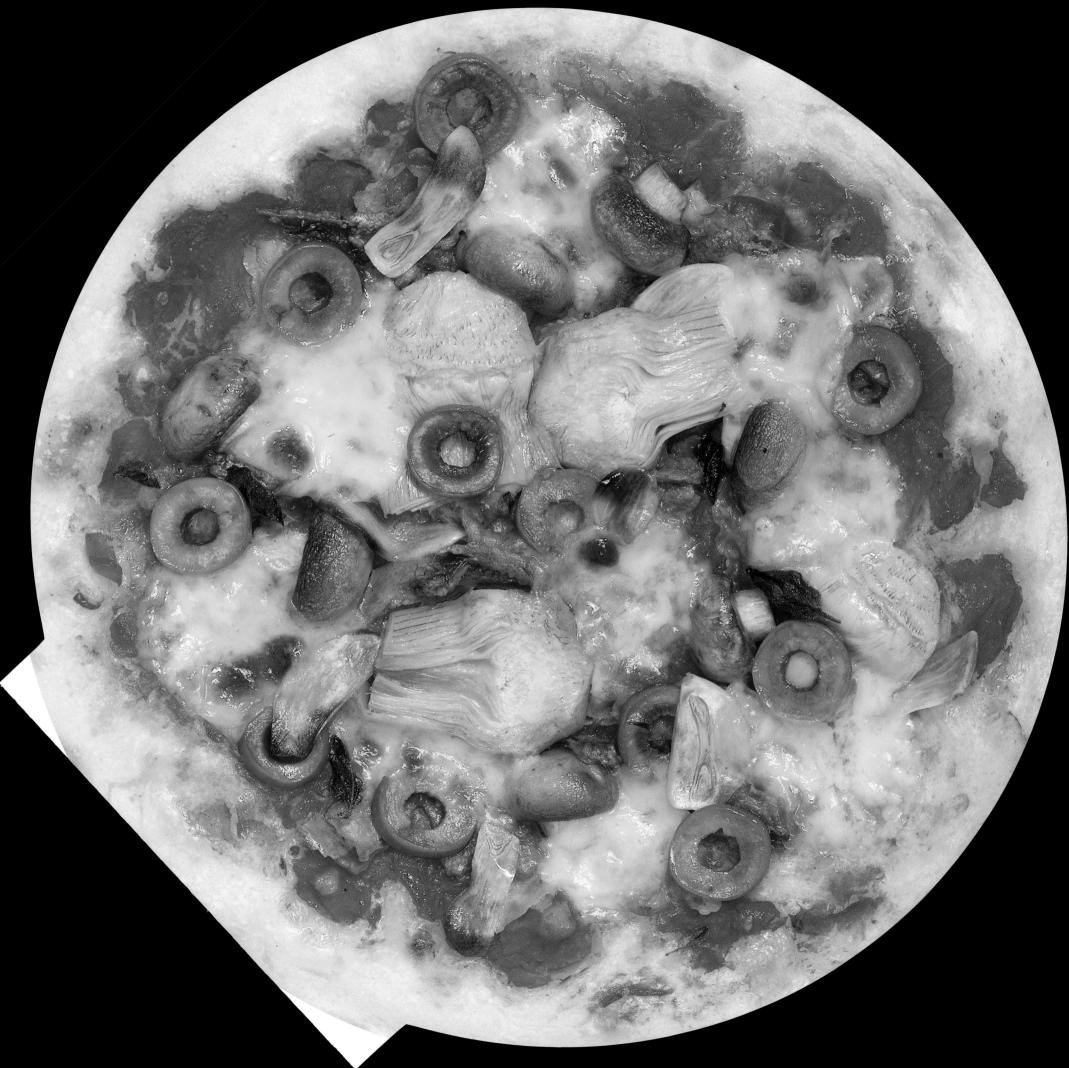

CRUST

Basic pizza dough (see pages 8–11)

TOPPING

8 ounces (250 g) porcini mushrooms (or white mushrooms), sliced
2 tablespoons extra-virgin olive oil · 1 tablespoon finely chopped fresh parsley
1 clove garlic, finely chopped · Salt and freshly ground black pepper

SERVES 2 · **PREPARATION** 15 MINUTES + TIME TO PREPARE THE DOUGH & LET RISE
COOKING 12–18 MINUTES

mushroom pizza

CRUST **1. Prepare** the pizza dough following the instructions on pages 8–11. Set aside to rise. **2. Oil** a 12-inch (30-cm) pizza pan. TOPPING **3. Sauté** the mushrooms in 1 tablespoon of oil over high heat until just tender, 2–3 minutes. Drain off any excess liquid and stir in the parsley and garlic. Set aside. **4. Preheat** the oven to 500°F (250°C/gas 10). **5. Knead** the risen pizza dough briefly on a lightly floured work surface, then press it into the prepared pan using your hands. **6. Spread** the mushrooms evenly over the dough, leaving a 1/2-inch (1-cm) border all around. Season with salt and pepper. Drizzle with the remaining 1 tablespoon of oil. **7. Bake** for 12–18 minutes, until the crust is crisp and golden brown. **8. Serve** hot.

Porcini mushrooms, also known as cèpes, grow wild across much of the Northern Hemisphere. They are widely appreciated for their delicious mushroomy flavor. Efforts to grow them commercially have not been successful. If they don't grow in your area, replace them in this recipe with another wild mushroom or with cultivated white mushrooms.

● If you liked this recipe, try the cheese pizza with ham & mushrooms on page 88.

four seasons
pizza

CRUST

Basic pizza dough (see pages 8–11)

TOPPING

2 tablespoons extra-virgin olive oil • 2–3 button mushrooms, sliced • Salt
1 cup (250 g) diced canned tomatoes, with juice • 3 ounces (90 g) artichoke hearts
in oil, drained and halved • 4–6 black olives • 2–3 salt-cured anchovy fillets, crumbled
6–8 mussels, shelled • 1 clove garlic, thinly sliced

SERVES 2 • PREPARATION 25 MINUTES + TIME TO PREPARE THE DOUGH & LET RISE
COOKING 15–20 MINUTES

CRUST **1. Prepare** the pizza dough following the instructions on pages 8–11. Set aside to rise. TOPPING **2. Heat** 1 tablespoon of oil in a small frying pan over medium heat. Add the mushrooms and sauté for 3–4 minutes. Season with salt and set aside. **3. Preheat** the oven to 500°F (250°C/gas 10). **4. Oil** a 12-inch (30-cm) pizza pan. **5. Knead** the risen pizza dough briefly on a lightly floured work surface, then press it into the prepared pan using your hands. **6. Spread** the tomatoes evenly over the dough, leaving a ½-inch (1-cm) border all around. **7. Now imagine** the pizza divided into 4 equal wedges: Garnish one quarter with mushrooms, one with artichokes, one with mussels and garlic, and one with olives and anchovies, until the crust is crisp and golden brown. **8. Bake** for 10–15 minutes, until the crust is crisp and golden brown. **9. Drizzle** with the remaining 1 tablespoon of oil. **10. Serve** hot.

44

• If you liked this recipe, try the artichoke pizza on page 60.

spicy 4-cheese
pizza

CRUST

Basic pizza dough (see pages 8–11)

TOPPING

2 ounces (60 g) mozzarella cheese, thinly sliced or shredded • 3 tablespoons freshly grated Parmesan cheese, thinly sliced cut in small cubes • 2 ounces (60 g) freshly grated Emmental cheese • 2 ounces (60 g) Gorgonzola cheese, 1 tablespoon extra-virgin olive oil • 1/2 teaspoon crushed dried chiles or red pepper flakes

SERVES 2 · PREPARATION 15 MINUTES + TIME TO PREPARE THE DOUGH & LET RISE · COOKING 10–15 MINUTES

CRUST **1. Prepare** the pizza dough following the instructions on pages 8–11. Set aside to rise. **2. Preheat** the oven to 500°F (250°C/gas 10). **3. Oil** a 12-inch (30-cm) pizza pan. **4. Knead** the risen pizza dough briefly on a lightly floured work surface, then press it into the prepared pan using your hands. TOPPING **5. Spread** the dough evenly with the cheeses, leaving a 1/2-inch (1-cm) border all around. Drizzle with the oil. **6. Bake** for 10–15 minutes, until the crust is crisp and golden brown and the cheeses are bubbling and beginning to brown. **7. Sprinkle** with the crushed chiles or red pepper flakes. **8. Serve** hot.

Omit the chilies or red pepper flakes, if desired. Add a little color by garnishing the cooked pizza with a few fresh cilantro (coriander) leaves.

● If you liked this recipe, try the two-cheese pizza on page 54.

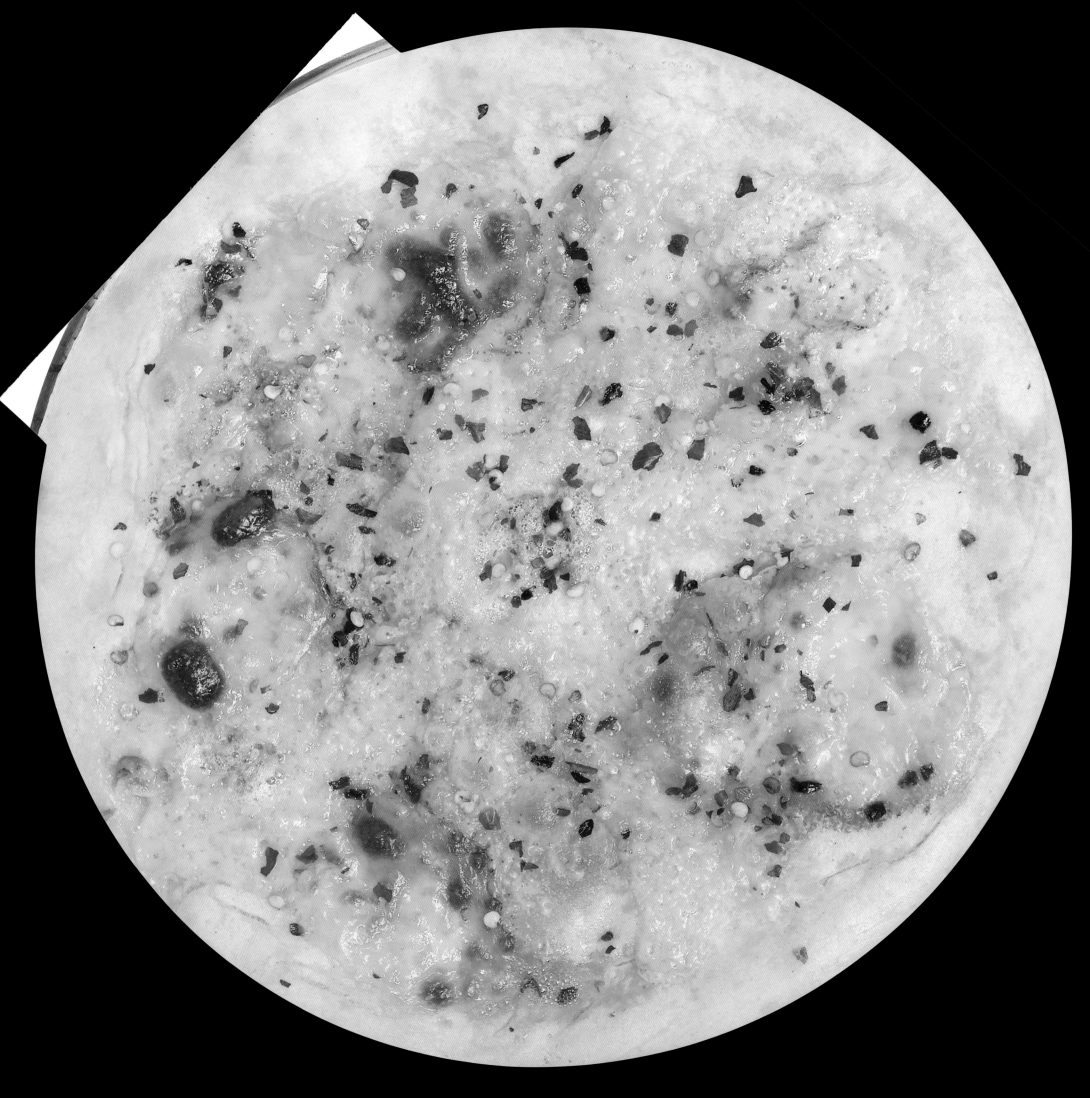

Sardinian pizza

SERVES 2 · PREPARATION 25 MINUTES + TIME TO PREPARE THE DOUGH & LET RISE
COOKING 10-15 MINUTES

CRUST

2 medium potatoes, peeled and cut in small cubes · 1 tablespoon lard, softened
Basic pizza dough (see pages 8–11)

TOPPING

4 ounces (120 g) mild pecorino, thinly sliced · 6 salt-cured anchovy fillets, rinsed and chopped · 3 medium tomatoes, peeled and chopped · 1/2 teaspoon dried oregano
Freshly ground black pepper · 1/3 cup (50 g) freshly grated aged pecorino (or Parmesan) cheese
1 tablespoon extra-virgin olive oil

CRUST **1. Cook** the potatoes in a small pot of salted boiling water until tender, about 10 minutes. Drain well and mash with the lard until smooth. Let cool slightly. **2. Prepare** the pizza dough following the instructions on pages 8–11, incorporating the potato and lard mixture as you knead. Set aside to rise. **3. Preheat** the oven to 500°F (250°C/gas 10). **4. Oil** a 12-inch (30-cm) pizza pan. **5. Knead** the risen pizza dough briefly on

a lightly floured work surface, then press it into the prepared pan using your hands. TOPPING **6. Cover** the dough evenly with the sliced pecorino, anchovies, and tomatoes. Sprinkle with the oregano and season with pepper. Top with the grated cheese and drizzle with the oil. **7. Bake** for 10-15 minutes, until the crust is crisp and golden brown and the cheeses are bubbling and beginning to brown. **8. Serve** hot.

The Mediterranean island of Sardinia produces some of the finest pecorino cheese in the world. This pizza makes the most of the island's gourmet resources.

● If you liked this recipe, try the Palermo-style pizza on page 50.

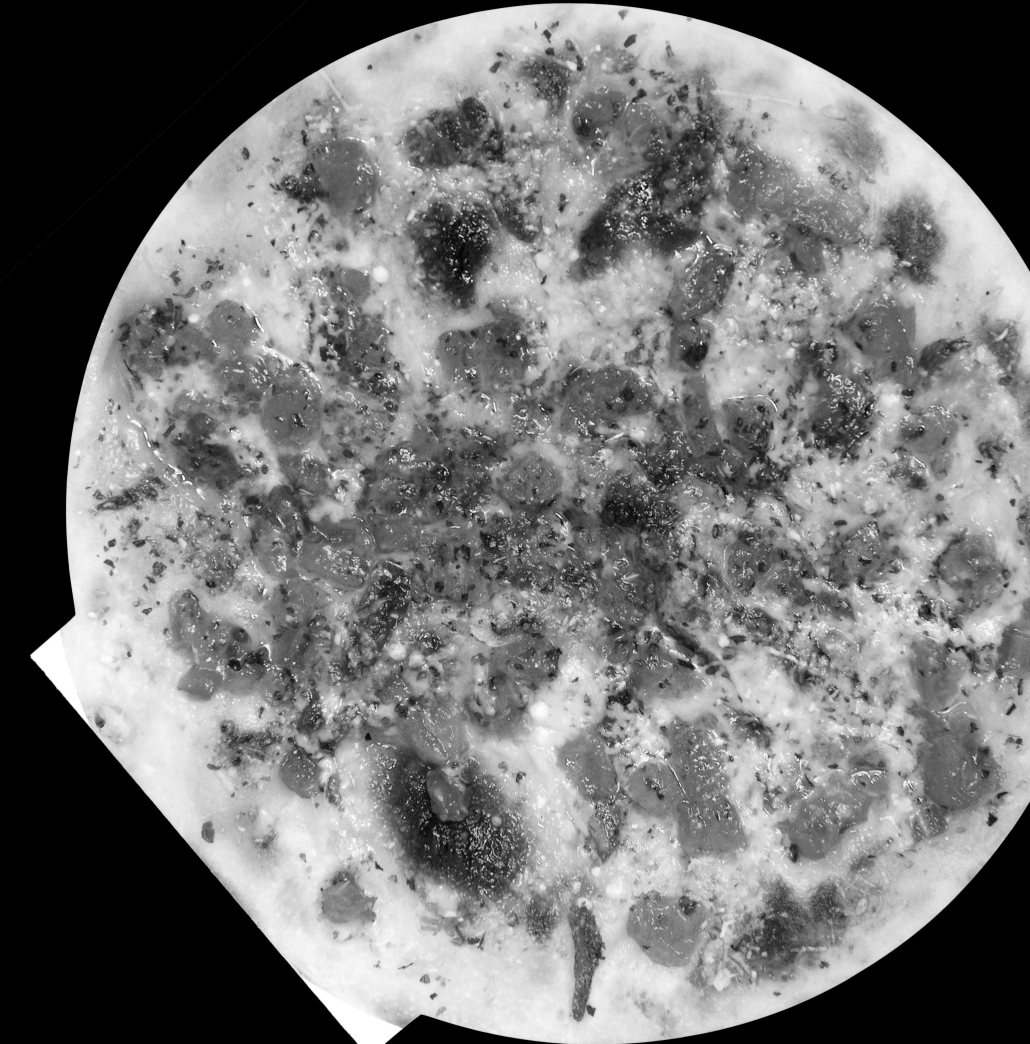

Palermo-style pizza

CRUST

Basic pizza dough (see pages 8–11)

TOPPING

⅓ cup (50 g) freshly grated pecorino cheese • 1 tablespoon extra-virgin olive oil • 1 tablespoon freshly squeezed lemon juice

6 tablespoons (90 ml) extra-virgin olive oil • 1 onion, finely chopped • 1 cup (250 g) diced canned tomatoes, with juice • 4 tablespoons finely chopped fresh parsley • 5 salt-cured anchovies, rinsed and chopped • 4 ounces (120 g) pecorino cheese, coarsely grated • ¼ cup (30 g) fresh bread crumbs

SERVES 2 • PREPARATION 30 MINUTES + TIME TO PREPARE THE DOUGH & LET RISE

COOKING 1 HOUR 20–25 MINUTES

CRUST 1. Prepare the pizza dough following the instructions on pages 8–11, incorporating the cheese, oil, and lemon juice into the dough as you mix it. Knead as usual and set aside to rise.

TOPPING 2. Heat ¼ cup (60 ml) of oil in a saucepan over medium heat. Add the onion and sauté until softened, 3–4 minutes. Add the tomatoes. Cover and simmer over low heat for 1 hour. **3. Add** the parsley, half the anchovies, and the pecorino. Simmer for 10 minutes. Set aside. **4. Preheat** the oven to 500°F (250°C/gas 10). **5. Oil** a 12-inch (30-cm) pizza pan. **6. Knead** the risen pizza dough briefly on a lightly floured work surface, then press it into the prepared pan using your hands. **7. Spread** evenly with half the sauce, leaving a ½-inch (1-cm) border all around. Bake for 5–8 minutes, until the base is almost cooked through. Add the remaining 2 tablespoons of oil in a small frying pan over medium heat. **8. Meanwhile,** heat the remaining sauce over the pizza. Sprinkle with the remaining anchovies and sautéed bread crumbs. Bake for 3–5 minutes, until the crust is crisp and golden brown. **9. Spread** the remaining anchovies and sauté until crisp and golden brown, 2–3 minutes. **10. Serve** hot.

● If you liked this recipe, try the Sicilian pizza on page 52.

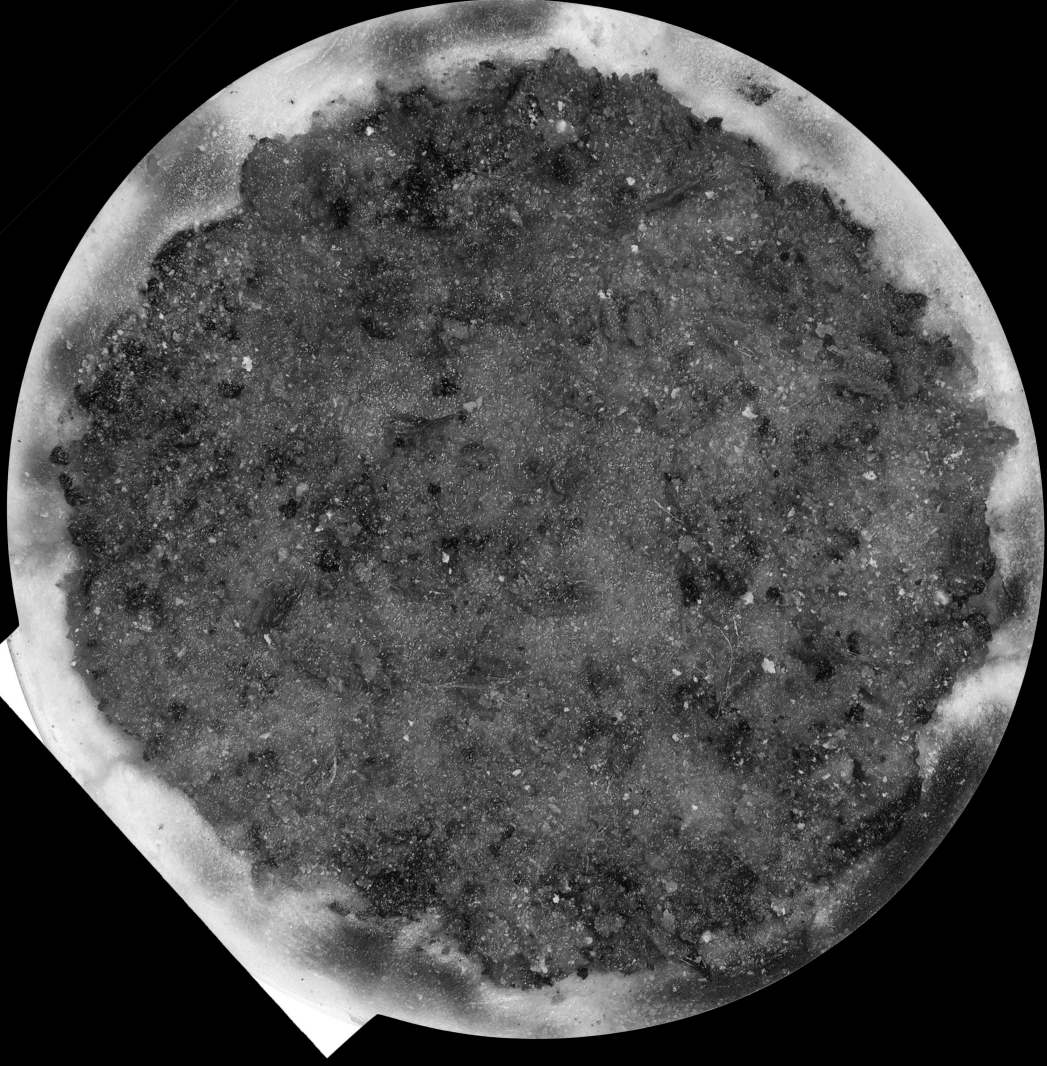

Sicilian pizza

CRUST

Basic pizza dough (see pages 8–11)

TOPPING

1½ cups (350 g) diced canned tomatoes, with juice • 6–8 fresh basil leaves + extra, to garnish • 12–15 black olives • 1 small onion, thinly sliced ½ cup (60 g) freshly grated pecorino cheese • 1 teaspoon finely chopped fresh oregano 4–6 anchovy fillets, crumbled • 2 tablespoons extra-virgin olive oil

SERVES 2 · **PREPARATION** 15 MINUTES + TIME TO PREPARE THE DOUGH & LET RISE **COOKING** 10–15 MINUTES

CRUST **1. Prepare** the pizza dough following the instructions on pages 8–11. Set aside to rise. **2. Preheat** the oven to 500°F (250°C/gas 10). **3. Oil** a 12-inch (30-cm) pizza pan. **4. Knead** the risen pizza dough briefly on a lightly floured work surface, then press it into the prepared pan using your hands. TOPPING **5. Spread** the dough evenly with the tomatoes, leaving a ½-inch (1-cm) border all around. Sprinkle with the basil, olives, onion, pecorino, and oregano. Finish with the anchovies and drizzle with 1 tablespoon of oil. **6. Bake** for 10–15 minutes, until the crust is crisp and golden brown and the cheese is bubbling and beginning to brown. **7. Drizzle** with the remaining 1 tablespoon of oil, garnish with the basil. **8. Serve** hot.

Traditional Sicilian pizza has a thicker, softer crust than pizza from northern Italy. It is not quite as thick as deep-dish pizza, but almost. Use the thicker crust (see page 8).

● **If you liked this recipe, try the pizza Napoletana on page 18.**

CRUST

Basic pizza dough (see pages 8–11)

TOPPING

½ cup (120 g) fresh ricotta cheese, drained · 3½ ounces (100 g) Gorgonzola cheese, diced · 2 tablespoons fresh chives, snipped
1 small clove garlic, finely chopped · 2 tablespoons heavy (double) cream
1 tablespoon extra-virgin olive oil

SERVES 2 · PREPARATION 15 MINUTES + TIME TO PREPARE THE DOUGH & LET RISE
COOKING 10–15 MINUTES

two-cheese pizza

CRUST **1. Prepare** the pizza dough following the instructions on pages 8–11. Set aside to rise. **2. Preheat** the oven to 500°F (250°C/gas 10). **3. Oil** a 12-inch (30-cm) pizza pan. **4. Knead** the risen pizza dough briefly on a lightly floured work surface, then press it into the prepared pan using your hands. TOPPING **5. Combine** the ricotta, Gorgonzola, 1 tablespoon of chives, garlic, cream, and oil in a bowl and mix well. **6. Spread** the topping evenly over the pizza, leaving a ½-inch (1-cm) border all around. **7. Bake** for 10–15 minutes, until the crust is crisp and golden brown and the cheeses are bubbling and beginning to brown. **8. Sprinkle** with the remaining 1 tablespoon of chives. **9. Serve** hot.

Ricotta is a grainy, sweet cheese made from the whey leftover when making other cheeses. It is very perishable and should only be used when very fresh.

54

● If you liked this recipe, try the whole-wheat pizza with 3-cheese topping on page 90.

eggplant pizza

CRUST

Basic pizza dough (see pages 8–11)

TOPPING

3–4 slices eggplant (aubergine), about ½-inch (1-cm) thick, with skin
3 tablespoons extra-virgin olive oil · Salt · 2 cloves garlic, finely chopped
1 tablespoon finely chopped fresh parsley · 1 cup (250 g) diced canned tomatoes, with juice
3½ ounces (100 g) mozzarella cheese, thinly sliced or shredded · Fresh basil, to garnish

SERVES 2 · PREPARATION 15 MINUTES + TIME TO PREPARE THE DOUGH & LET RISE
COOKING 25–30 MINUTES

CRUST **1. Prepare** the pizza dough following the instructions on pages 8–11. Set aside to rise. TOPPING **2. Brush** the eggplant with 2 tablespoons of oil. Grill in a hot grill pan, turning once, until tender and lined with black grill marks. Sprinkle with salt, garlic, and parsley. Set aside. **3. Preheat** the oven to 500°F (250°C/gas 10). **4. Oil** a 12-inch (30-cm) pizza pan. **5. Knead** the risen pizza dough briefly on a lightly floured work surface, then press it into the prepared pan using your hands. **6. Spread** the tomatoes evenly over the crust, leaving a ½-inch (1-cm) border all around. Sprinkle with the mozzarella. Cover with the slices of eggplant. Drizzle with the remaining 1 tablespoon of oil. **7. Bake** for 10–15 minutes, until the crust is crisp and golden brown and the cheese is bubbling and beginning to brown. **8. Garnish** with the basil. **9. Serve** hot.

Grilled eggplant has a rich, almost sweet flavor. There is no need to remove the skin, because it will soften during grilling and baking.

• If you liked this recipe, try the pizza with beef, zucchini & eggplant on page 86.

56

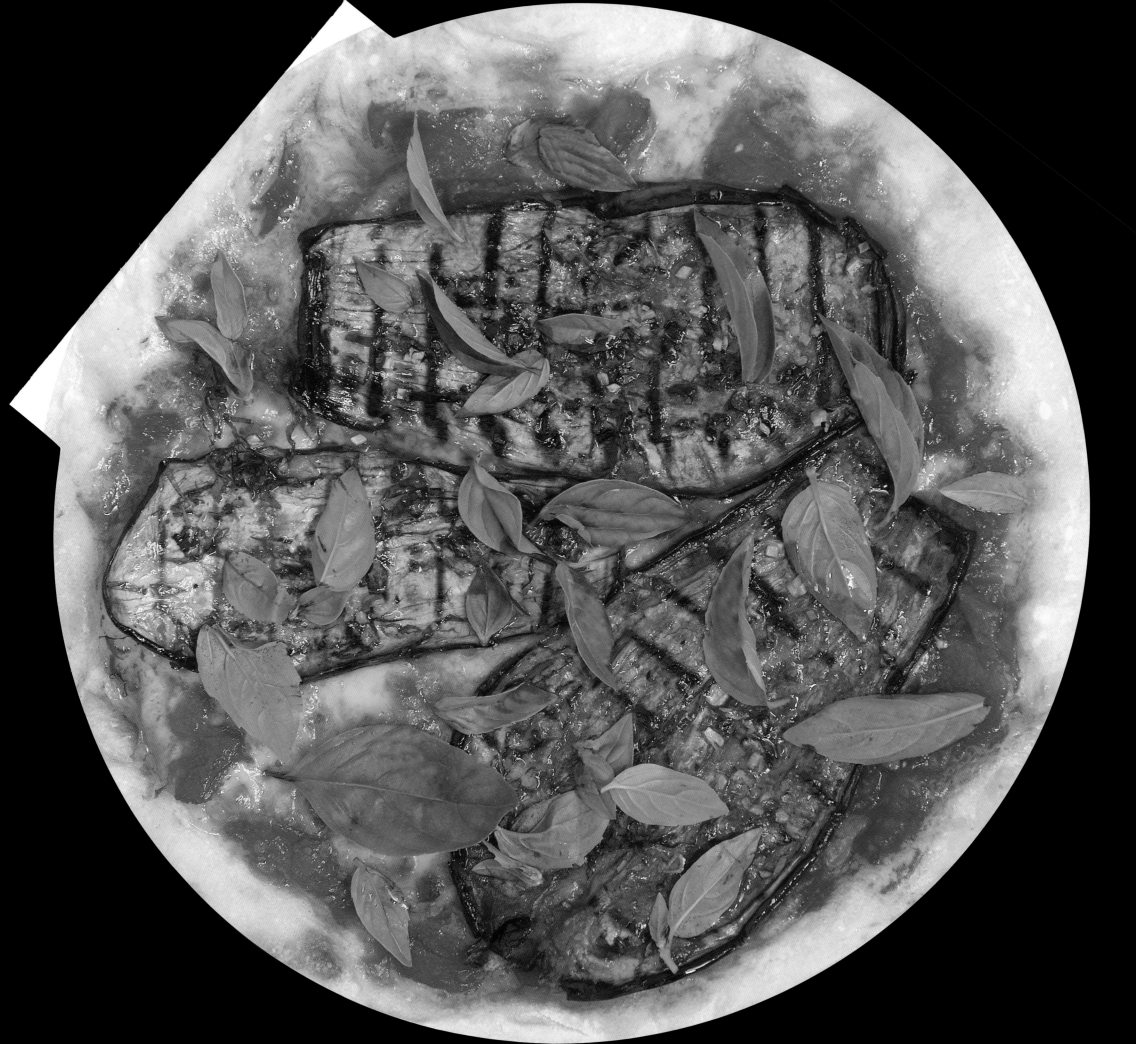

bell pepper pizza

CRUST

Basic pizza dough (see pages 8–11)

TOPPING

3 tablespoons extra-virgin olive oil • 1 small red bell pepper (capsicum), cut in strips • 1 small yellow bell pepper (capsicum), cut in strips • 1 cup (250 g) diced canned tomatoes, with juice • 1 tablespoon capers in brine, drained • Salt • 4 ounces (120 g) mozzarella cheese, thinly sliced or shredded

SERVES 2 • **PREPARATION** 25 MINUTES + TIME TO PREPARE THE DOUGH & LET RISE • **COOKING** 20–25 MINUTES

CRUST 1. Prepare the pizza dough following the instructions on pages 8–11. Set aside to rise. **TOPPING 2. Heat** 2 tablespoons of oil in a medium frying pan over medium heat. Sauté the onion and bell peppers for 5 minutes. Add the tomatoes and capers. Season with salt and simmer, stirring often, until the bell peppers have wilted and the tomatoes have reduced a little, 5–7 minutes. **3. Preheat** the oven to 500°F (250°C/gas 10). **4. Oil** a 12-inch (30-cm) pizza pan. **5. Knead** the risen pizza dough briefly on a lightly floured work surface, then press it into the prepared pan using your hands. **6. Spread** the bell pepper mixture evenly over the crust, leaving a ½-inch (1-cm) border all around. Sprinkle with the cheese and drizzle with the remaining 1 tablespoon of oil. **7. Bake** for 10–15 minutes, until the crust is crisp and golden brown and the cheese is bubbling and beginning to brown. **8. Serve** hot.

This is a classic Italian pizza and many believe it was the first pizza ever made. You can vary it by adding olives, capers, or garlic.

● If you liked this recipe, try the pizza with ratatouille & olives on page 68.

artichoke pizza

CRUST

Basic pizza dough (see pages 8–11)

TOPPING

2 artichokes · Freshly squeezed juice of ½ lemon
2 tablespoons extra-virgin olive oil · Salt and freshly ground black pepper
4 ounces (120 g) Fontina cheese, very thinly sliced

SERVES 2 · PREPARATION 25 MINUTES + TIME TO PREPARE THE DOUGH & LET RISE
COOKING 15–20 MINUTES

CRUST **1. Prepare** the pizza dough following the instructions on pages 8–11. Set aside to rise.

TOPPING **2. Clean** the artichokes by trimming the stalks and removing tough outer leaves. Trim off and discard the top third of the leaves. Cut each one in half and remove any fuzzy inner choke with a sharp knife. Put in a bowl of cold water with the lemon juice for 10 minutes. **3. Drain** the artichokes, pat dry with paper towels, and slice thinly. **4. Heat** the oil in a large frying pan over medium heat. Add the artichokes and sauté until tender, about 5 minutes. Season with salt. **5. Preheat** the oven to 500°F (250°C/gas 10). **6. Oil** a 12-inch (30-cm) pizza pan. **7. Knead** the risen pizza dough briefly on a lightly floured work surface, then press it into the prepared pan using your hands. **8. Spread** the dough with the artichokes, leaving a ½-inch (1-cm) border all around. Season with salt and pepper and cover with the cheese. **9. Bake** for 10–15 minutes, until the crust is crisp and golden brown and the cheese is bubbling and beginning to brown. **10. Serve** hot.

Artichokes belong to the thistle family and originally come from the Mediterranean. They are often used in Italian cuisine.

● If you liked this recipe, try the whole-wheat pizza with 3-cheese topping on page 90.

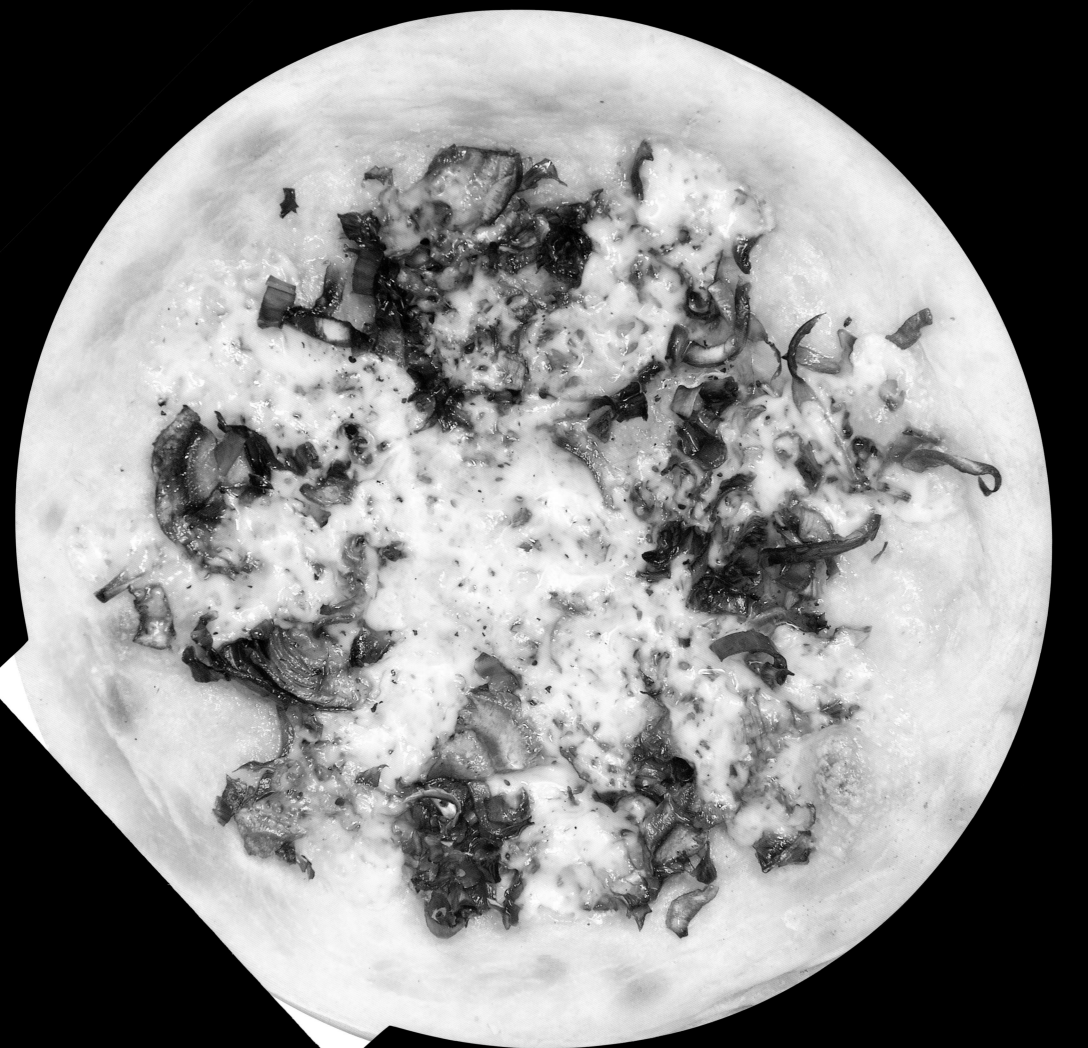

pizza with leeks

CRUST

Basic pizza dough (see pages 8–11)

TOPPING

2 tablespoons butter · 2 leeks, thinly sliced · 3 ounces (90 g) pancetta, diced
Salt and freshly ground black pepper · 1 egg · 1½ tablespoons
fresh cream · 4 tablespoons freshly grated Parmesan cheese
2 ounces (60 g) Gruyère cheese, very thinly sliced

SERVES 2 · **PREPARATION** 20 MINUTES + TIME TO PREPARE THE DOUGH & LET RISE
COOKING 20–25 MINUTES

CRUST **1. Prepare** the pizza dough following the instructions on pages 8–11. Set aside to rise. TOPPING **2. Melt** the butter in a small frying pan over medium heat. Add the leeks and pancetta and sauté until the leeks are tender, about 10 minutes. Season with salt and pepper and set aside. **3. Preheat** the oven to 500°F (250°C/gas 10). **4. Oil** a 12-inch (30-cm) pizza pan. **5. Knead** the risen pizza dough briefly on a lightly floured work surface, then press it into the prepared pan using your hands. **6. Beat** the egg with the cream in a bowl. Add the leek and pancetta mixture and the two cheeses. Mix well. **7. Spread** this mixture evenly over the pizza, leaving a ½-inch (1-cm) border all around. **8. Bake** for 10–15 minutes, until the crust is crisp and golden brown and the topping is bubbling and beginning to brown. **9. Serve** hot.

The sweet, onion flavor of the leeks blends in beautifully with the pancetta and cheese in this delicious pizza.

● If you liked this recipe, try the pizza with onion & pesto on page 24.

white pizza
with **prosciutto & arugula**

CRUST

Basic pizza dough (see pages 8–11)

TOPPING

1 tablespoon extra-virgin olive oil · 4 ounces (120 g) mozzarella cheese, thinly sliced or shredded · 2 ounces (60 g) prosciutto, very thinly sliced

Small bunch fresh arugula (rocket)

SERVES 2 · **PREPARATION** 10 MINUTES + TIME TO PREPARE THE DOUGH & LET RISE

COOKING 10–15 MINUTES

CRUST **1. Prepare** the pizza dough following the instructions on pages 8–11. Set aside to rise. **2. Preheat** the oven to 500°F (250°C/gas 10). **3. Oil** a 12-inch (30-cm) pizza pan. **4. Knead** the risen pizza dough briefly on a lightly floured work surface, then press it into the prepared pan using your hands.

TOPPING **5. Brush** the dough with the oil. Cover with the mozzarella and top with the prosciutto, leaving a ½-inch (1-cm) border all around. **6. Bake** for 10–15 minutes, until the crust is crisp and golden brown and the cheese is bubbling and beginning to brown. **7. Top** with the arugula. **8. Serve** hot.

• If you liked this recipe, try the pizza bianca on page 30.

64

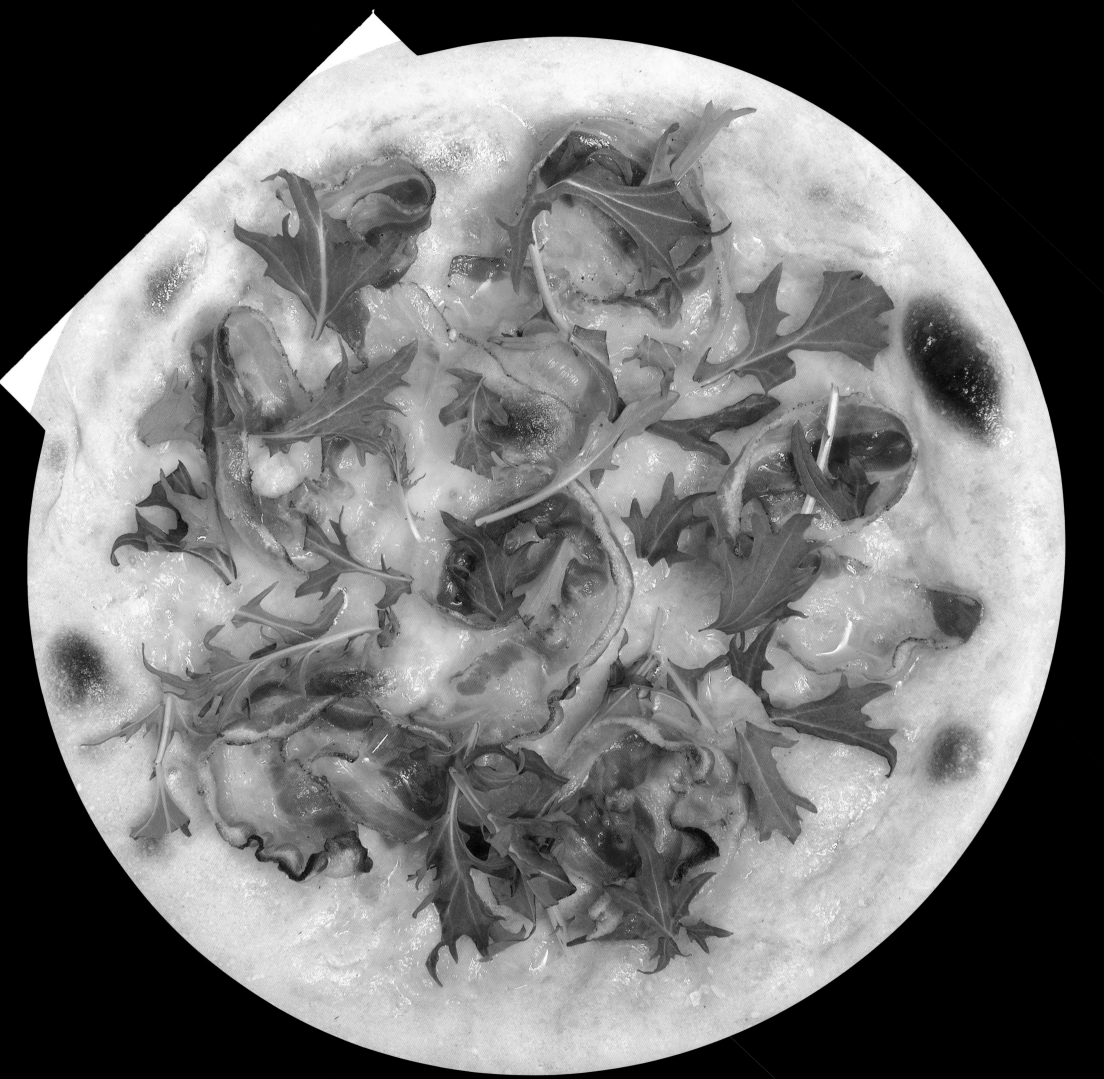

pizza with sausage & mushrooms

CRUST

Basic pizza dough (see pages 8–11)

TOPPING

2 tablespoons extra-virgin olive oil • 2 small onions, thinly sliced
8 ounces (250 g) Italian sausages, casing discarded and sliced • 5 ounces (150 g)
button mushrooms, sliced • Salt and freshly ground black pepper • 1 cup (250 g) diced
canned tomatoes, with juice • 3½ ounces (100 g) mozzarella cheese, thinly sliced or shredded
5 cherry tomatoes, halved

SERVES 2 • **PREPARATION** 15 MINUTES + TIME TO PREPARE THE DOUGH & LET RISE
COOKING 20–25 MINUTES

CRUST 1. Prepare the pizza dough following the instructions on pages 8–11. Set aside to rise. **2. Preheat** the oven to 500°F (250°C/gas 10). **3. Oil** a 12-inch (30-cm) pizza pan. **TOPPING 4. Heat** the oil in a large frying pan over medium heat. Add the onions and sauté until transparent, 3–4 minutes. Add the sausage and mushrooms and sauté until the sausage is browned, about 5 minutes. Season with salt and

pepper. **5. Knead** the risen pizza dough briefly on a lightly floured work surface, then press it into the prepared pan using your hands. **6. Spread** the tomato evenly over the dough, leaving a ½-inch (1-cm) border all around. Top with the sausage mixture, mozzarella, and cherry tomatoes. **7. Bake** for 10–15 minutes, until the crust is crisp and golden brown and the cheese is bubbling and beginning to brown. **8. Serve** hot.

This is a hearty pizza that can be served as a meal in itself. It is best made with the thick crust (see page 8).

• If you liked this recipe, try the pizza with tomato, garlic & sausage on page 106.

66

pizza with ratatouille & olives

CRUST

Basic pizza dough (see pages 8–11)

TOPPING

1 large eggplant, cut into small cubes • Salt • 1 pound (500 g) ripe tomatoes
3 tablespoons extra-virgin olive oil • 2 small onions, thinly sliced
1 clove garlic, thinly sliced • 1 tablespoon finely chopped fresh parsley • 1 red bell pepper
(capsicum), seeded and cut in small squares • 2 small zucchini (courgettes), sliced
6–8 green olives, halved • Freshly ground black pepper • 1 tablespoon finely chopped fresh thyme

SERVES 2 • PREPARATION 25 MINUTES + TIME TO PREPARE THE DOUGH & LET RISE
COOKING 25–35 MINUTES

CRUST **1. Prepare** the pizza dough following the instructions on pages 8–11. Set aside to rise. TOPPING **2. Place** the eggplant in a colander. Sprinkle with salt and let rest for 30 minutes. **3. Rinse** the eggplant and drain well. **4. Blanch** the tomatoes in boiling water for 30 seconds. Drain and slip off the skins. Slice thickly. **5. Heat** 2 tablespoons of oil in a medium saucepan over medium heat. Add the onions, garlic, parsley, eggplant, bell peppers, tomatoes, and zucchini and simmer until tender,

15–20 minutes. Stir frequently. **6. Preheat** the oven to 500°F (250°C/gas 10). **7. Oil** a 12-inch (30-cm) pizza pan. **8. Knead** the risen pizza dough briefly on a lightly floured work surface, then press it into the prepared pan using your hands. **9. Spread** the ratatouille evenly over the dough, leaving a ½-inch (1-cm) border all around. Sprinkle with the olives. Season with salt and pepper. **10. Bake** for 10–15 minutes, until the crust is crisp and golden brown. **11. Sprinkle** with the thyme and drizzle with the remaining oil. **12. Serve** hot.

Ratatouille is a French vegetable stew. The quantity you prepare for this recipe will be enough to top two pizzas.

• If you liked this recipe, try the whole-wheat pizza with vegetable topping on page 96.

pizza with spicy salami

CRUST
Basic pizza dough (see pages 8–11)

TOPPING
1 cup (250 g) diced canned tomatoes, with juice · 3½ ounces (100 g) spicy hard salami or pepperoni, thinly sliced · 1 onion, very thinly sliced · 4 ounces (120 g) mozzarella cheese, thinly sliced or shredded · 1 tablespoon extra-virgin olive oil · ½ teaspoon dried oregano

SERVES 2 · **PREPARATION** 15 MINUTES + TIME TO PREPARE THE DOUGH & LET RISE
COOKING 10–15 MINUTES

CRUST **1. Prepare** the pizza dough following the instructions on pages 8–11. Set aside to rise. **2. Preheat** the oven to 500°F (250°C/gas 10). **3. Oil** a 12-inch (30-cm) pizza pan. **4. Knead** the risen pizza dough briefly on a lightly floured work surface, then press it into the prepared pan using your hands.

TOPPING **5. Spread** the tomatoes evenly over the dough, leaving a ½-inch (1-cm) border all around. Cover with the salami, onion, and mozzarella. Drizzle with the oil. **6. Bake** for 10–15 minutes, until the base is crisp and golden brown and the mozzarella is bubbling and beginning to brown. **7. Sprinkle** with oregano. **8. Serve** hot.

In Italy, most spicy salami is made in the South, in the Campania and Calabria regions. It can be very fiery. Replace with a milder, local salami, if preferred.

• If you liked this recipe, try the pizza with pepperoni, mushrooms & fennel on page 104.

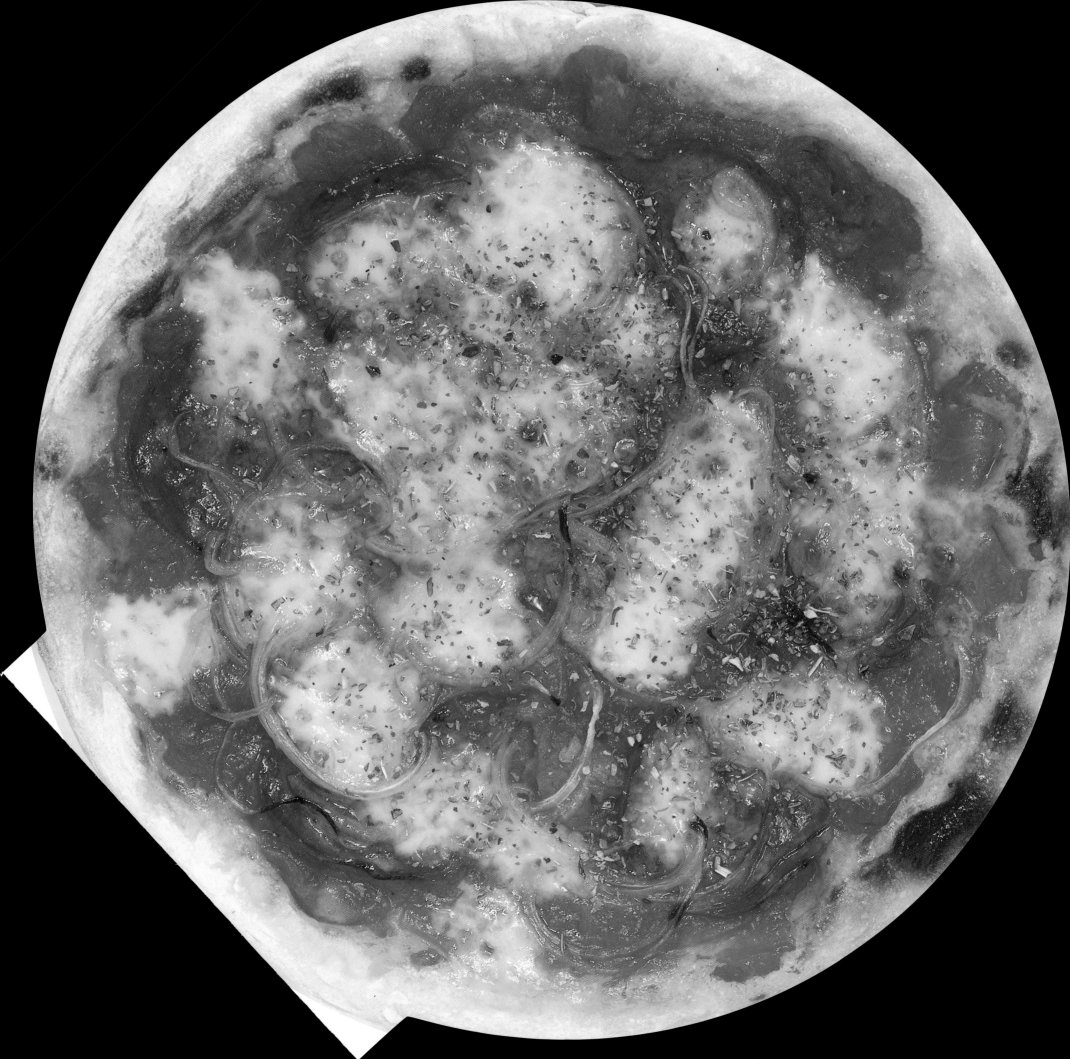

CRUST

Basic pizza dough (see pages 8–11)
12 ounces (350 g) potatoes, peeled
2 tablespoons extra-virgin olive oil

TOPPING

2 tablespoons extra-virgin olive oil · 1 clove garlic, finely chopped · 5 ounces (150 g) white
mushrooms, sliced · Salt and freshly ground black pepper · 1 teaspoon finely chopped fresh thyme
4 ounces (120 g) mozzarella cheese, thinly sliced or shredded · 1 tablespoon finely chopped fresh parsley

SERVES 2 · **PREPARATION** 25 MINUTES + TIME TO PREPARE THE DOUGH & LET RISE
COOKING 35–40 MINUTES

potato pizza
with **mushrooms**

CRUST **1. Cook** the potatoes in a large pot of salted boiling water until tender, about 25 minutes. Mash half the potatoes and thinly slice the rest. **2. Prepare** the pizza dough following the instructions on pages 8–11, incorporating the mashed potatoes and oil into the dough as you knead. Set aside to rise for 2 hours. **3. Preheat** the oven to 500°F (250°C/gas 10). **4. Oil** a 12-inch (30-cm) pizza pan. TOPPING **5. Heat** the oil in a large frying pan over medium heat. Add the garlic and sauté until pale gold, 2–3 minutes. Add the mushrooms and sauté until tender, about 5 minutes. Season with salt and pepper. Stir in the thyme. **6. Knead** the risen pizza dough briefly on a lightly floured work surface, then press it into the prepared pan using your hands. **7. Spread** the sliced potatoes, mozzarella, and mushroom mixture over the dough, leaving a ½-inch (1-cm) border all around. **8. Bake** for 10–15 minutes, until the crust is crisp and golden brown and the cheese is bubbling and beginning to brown. **9. Garnish** with parsley. **10. Serve** hot.

The addition of potatoes to the crust makes it softer and more breadlike.

● If you liked this recipe, try the pizza with cherry tomatoes & oregano on page 20.

pizza with artichokes & pancetta

CRUST

Basic pizza dough (see pages 8–11)
4 ounces (125 g) frozen puff pastry, thawed • Salt
2 tablespoons extra-virgin olive oil

TOPPING

1–2 artichokes • Freshly squeezed juice of 1/2 a lemon • Salt • 1/4 cup (60 ml) extra-virgin olive oil
2 ounces (60 g) pancetta, thinly sliced • 1 clove garlic, finely chopped
2 tablespoons dry white wine • 1 onion, thinly sliced • 1 teaspoon sugar

SERVES 2 • PREPARATION 1 HOUR + TIME TO PREPARE THE DOUGH & LET RISE
COOKING 35–50 MINUTES

CRUST **1. Prepare** the pizza dough following the instructions on pages 8–11. Set aside to rise. **2. Oil** a 12-inch (30-cm) pizza pan. TOPPING **3. Clean** the artichokes by removing the stalks and tough outer leaves. Trim off and discard the top third of the leaves. Cut each in half and remove the fuzzy inner choke with a sharp knife. Put in a bowl of cold water with the lemon juice. **4. Knead** the risen pizza dough briefly on a lightly floured work surface, then roll into an 8-inch (20-cm) disk. Put the puff pastry in the center and wrap the pizza dough around it. Roll out into a 5 x 14-inch (13 x 35-cm) strip. Fold the ends in toward the center. Roll out again to the same size as before. Fold the ends of the strip in again and repeat the process. Chill for 20 minutes. Repeat the rolling and folding process again three times. Chill for 20 minutes. **5. Preheat** the oven to 500°F (250°C/gas 10). **6. Roll** the dough out again. Repeat the folding process, then roll out into a 12-inch (30-cm) disk and place in the prepared pizza pan. Season with salt and drizzle with the oil. **7. Bake** for 10–15 minutes, until crisp and golden brown. Keep warm. **8. Heat** 1 tablespoon of oil in a small frying pan over medium heat. Add the pancetta and sauté until lightly browned and crisp, 3–4 minutes. Set aside. **9. Drain** the artichokes, pat dry, and slice thinly. Heat 2 tablespoons of oil in a large frying pan over medium heat. Add the artichokes, garlic, and wine. Simmer until the artichokes are tender, 10–15 minutes. **10. Heat** the remaining 1 tablespoon oil in a small frying pan over medium heat. Add the onion and sauté until tender, 2–3 minutes. Add the sugar, cover, and simmer over low heat until caramelized, 10–15 minutes. **11. Spread** the crust with the onion and top with the artichokes and pancetta. **12. Serve** hot.

• If you liked this recipe, try the pizza with leeks on page 62.

74

pizza with
apple & Gorgonzola

CRUST

Basic pizza dough (see pages 8–11)

TOPPING

4 ounces (120 g) Gorgonzola cheese • 3½ ounces (100 g) mozzarella cheese, thinly sliced or shredded • 1 Granny Smith apple, peeled, cored, and thinly sliced

Salt and freshly ground black pepper • 1 tablespoon extra-virgin olive oil

Fresh cilantro (coriander) leaves, to garnish

SERVES 2 • PREPARATION 15 MINUTES + TIME TO PREPARE THE DOUGH & LET RISE

COOKING 10–15 MINUTES

CRUST **1. Prepare** the pizza dough following the instructions on pages 8–11. Set aside to rise. **2. Preheat** the oven to 500°F (250°C/gas 10). **3.** Oil a 12-inch (30-cm) pizza pan. TOPPING **4. Mash** the Gorgonzola in a bowl using a fork until smooth and creamy. **5. Knead** the risen pizza dough briefly on a lightly floured work surface, then press it into the prepared pan using your hands. **6. Cover** the dough with slices of mozzarella, leaving a ½-inch (1-cm) border all around. Top with the apple and spread with the Gorgonzola. Season with salt and pepper. Drizzle with the oil. **7. Bake** for 10–15 minutes, until the crust is crisp and golden brown and the cheese is beginning to brown. **8. Garnish** with cilantro. **9. Serve** hot.

Another option is to replace the Gorgonzola with Roquefort or Stilton.

● If you liked this recipe, try the cheese pizza with onion, apple & walnuts on page 26.

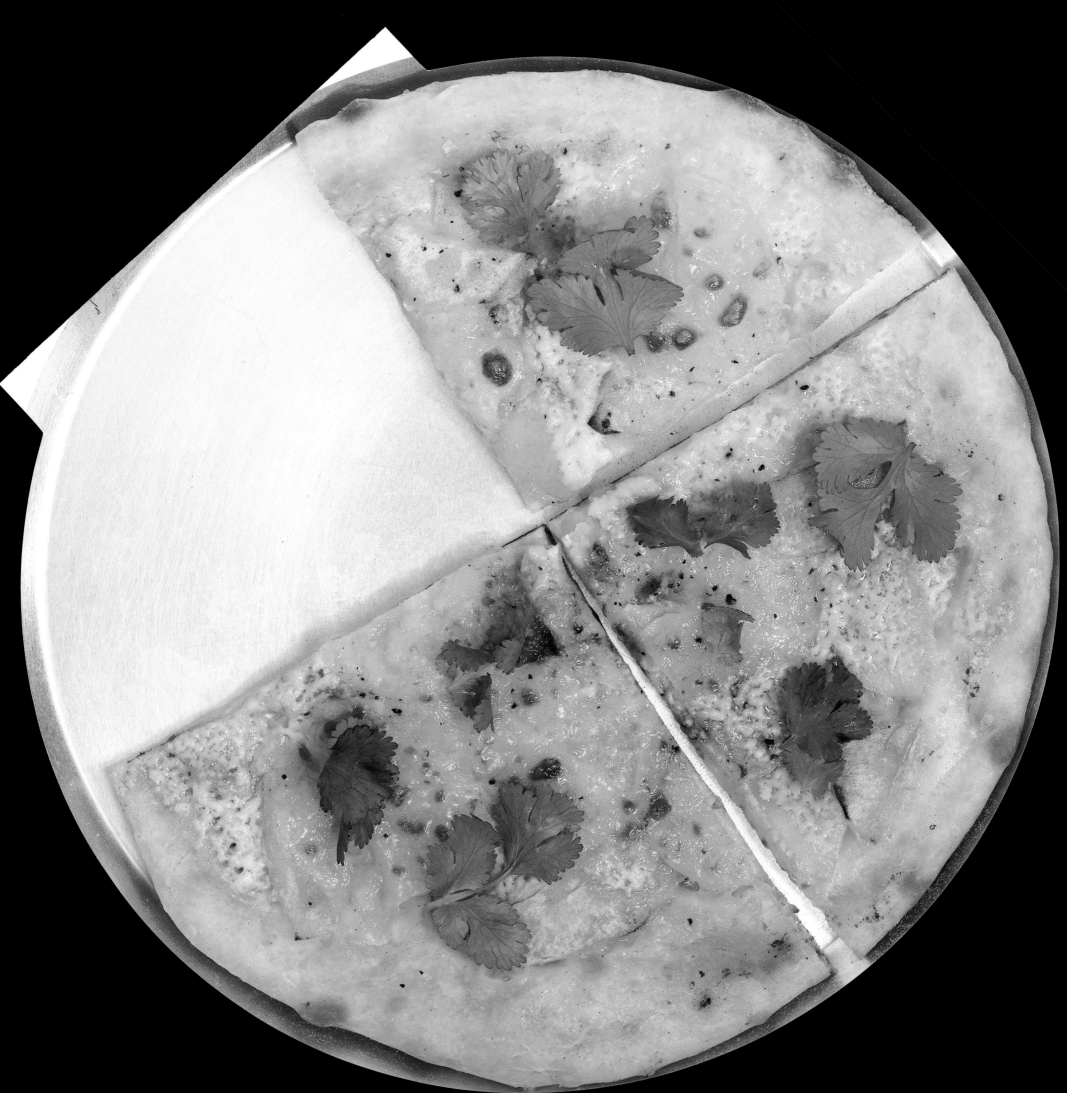

pizza with
ground beef & onions

CRUST

Basic pizza dough (see pages 8–11)

TOPPING

2 tablespoons extra-virgin olive oil · 2 medium onions, thinly sliced · 3 tomatoes, sliced · 2 tablespoons finely chopped fresh basil · Salt and freshly ground black pepper · 12 ounces (350 g) lean ground (minced) beef · ⅓ cup (90 ml) beef stock

SERVES 2 · **PREPARATION** 20 MINUTES + TIME TO PREPARE THE DOUGH & LET RISE · **COOKING** 40–55 MINUTES

CRUST **1. Prepare** the pizza dough following the instructions on pages 8–11. Set aside to rise. **2. Preheat** the oven to 500°F (250°C/gas 10). **3. Oil** a 12-inch (30-cm) pizza pan. TOPPING **4. Heat** 1 tablespoon of oil in a large frying pan over medium heat. Add the onions and sauté until transparent, 3–4 minutes. Remove from the pan and set aside. **5. Put** the tomatoes and basil in the same pan and sauté over medium heat until the tomatoes begin to break down, about 10 minutes. Season with salt and pepper. Remove from the pan and set aside. **6. Heat** the remaining 1 tablespoon of oil in the same pan over high heat. Add the meat and sauté until browned, 5–7 minutes. Add the stock and season with pepper. Lower the heat and simmer until the meat is cooked and most of the liquid has evaporated, 10–15 minutes. **7. Preheat** the oven to 500°F (250°C/gas 10). **8. Knead** the risen pizza dough briefly on a lightly floured work surface, then press it into the prepared pan using your hands. **9. Spread** with the tomato mixture followed by the meat mixture, leaving a ½-inch (1-cm) border all around. Top with the onions. **10. Bake** for 10–15 minutes, until the crust is crisp and golden brown. **11. Serve** hot.

• If you liked this recipe, try the pizza with beef, zucchini & eggplant on page 86.

78

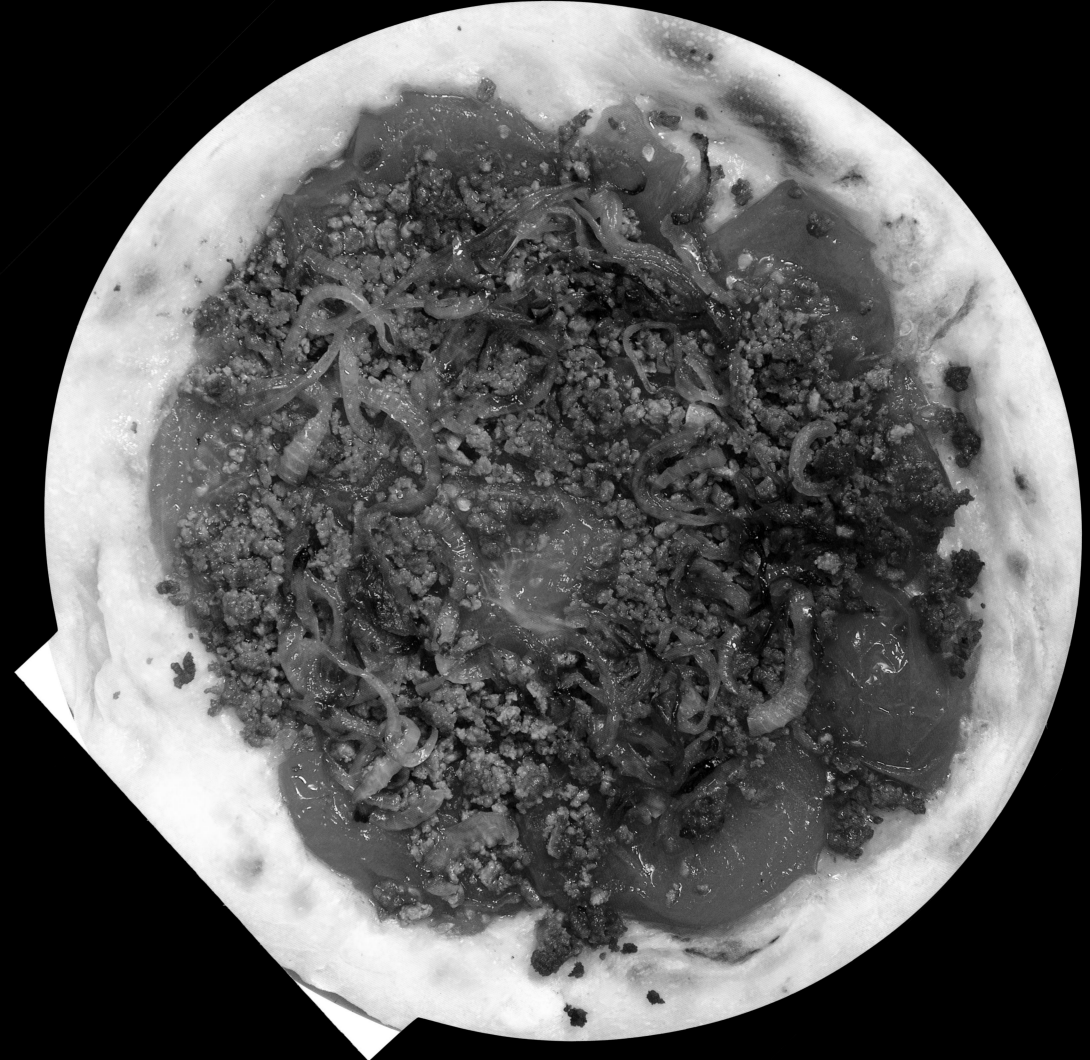

pizza with tuna & peas

CRUST

Basic pizza dough (see pages 8–11)

TOPPING

2 tablespoons extra-virgin olive oil • 1 large onion, sliced • Salt
1 cup (250 g) diced canned tomatoes, with juice • 3 ounces (90 g) canned tuna,
packed in water, drained and crumbled • ½ cup (75 g) frozen peas • 1 tablespoon capers
preserved in brine, drained • 4 ounces (100 g) mozzarella cheese, thinly sliced or shredded
Freshly ground black pepper

SERVES 2 • PREPARATION 15 MINUTES + TIME TO PREPARE THE DOUGH & LET RISE
COOKING 25–30 MINUTES

CRUST **1. Prepare** the pizza dough following the instructions on pages 8–11. Set aside to rise. **2. Preheat** the oven to 500°F (250°C/gas 10). **3. Oil** a 12-inch (30-cm) pizza pan. TOPPING **4. Heat** the oil in a medium saucepan over medium heat. Add the onion and sauté until transparent, 3–4 minutes. Season with salt. Add the tomatoes and simmer for 10 minutes. Stir in the tuna and peas and simmer for 2 minutes. **5. Knead** the risen pizza dough briefly on a lightly floured work surface, then press it into the pan using your hands. **6. Spread** the dough evenly with the tomato mixture, leaving a ½-inch (1-cm) border all around. Sprinkle with the capers and top with the mozzarella. Season with pepper. **7. Bake** for 10–15 minutes, until the crust is crisp and golden brown and the cheese is bubbling and beginning to brown. **8. Serve** hot.

• If you liked this recipe, try the seafood pizza on page 122.

pizza with sun-dried tomatoes

CRUST

Basic pizza dough (see pages 8–11)

TOPPING

¼ cup (60 ml) extra-virgin olive oil · 1 small eggplant (aubergine), sliced
2 ounces (60 g) sun-dried tomatoes, soaked in warm water for 20 minutes, drained
and coarsely chopped · 2 ounces (60 g) ham, chopped · 1 teaspoon finely chopped
fresh thyme, to garnish · 1 sprig fresh basil, to garnish

SERVES 2 · PREPARATION 30 MINUTES + TIME TO PREPARE THE DOUGH & LET RISE
COOKING 15–25 MINUTES

CRUST **1. Prepare** the pizza dough following the
instructions on pages 8–11. Set aside to rise.
2. Preheat the oven to 500°F (250°C/gas
10). **3. Oil** a 12-inch (30-cm) pizza pan.
TOPPING **4. Heat** the oil in a large
frying pan over medium heat. Add the
eggplant and fry until tender, 5–10
minutes. Drain on paper towels.
5. Knead the risen pizza dough briefly on
a lightly floured work surface, then press
it into the prepared pan using your
hands. **6. Arrange** the eggplant, sun-
dried tomatoes, and ham on the
dough, leaving a ½-inch (1-cm) border
all around. **7. Bake** for 10–15
minutes, until the crust is crisp and
golden brown. **8. Garnish** with the
thyme and basil. **9. Serve** hot.

*Sun-dried tomatoes were first made
in Italy as a way to preserve tomatoes
for the winter months. They are readily
available in supermarkets
and gourmet food stores.*

• If you liked this recipe, try the pizza margherita on page 14.

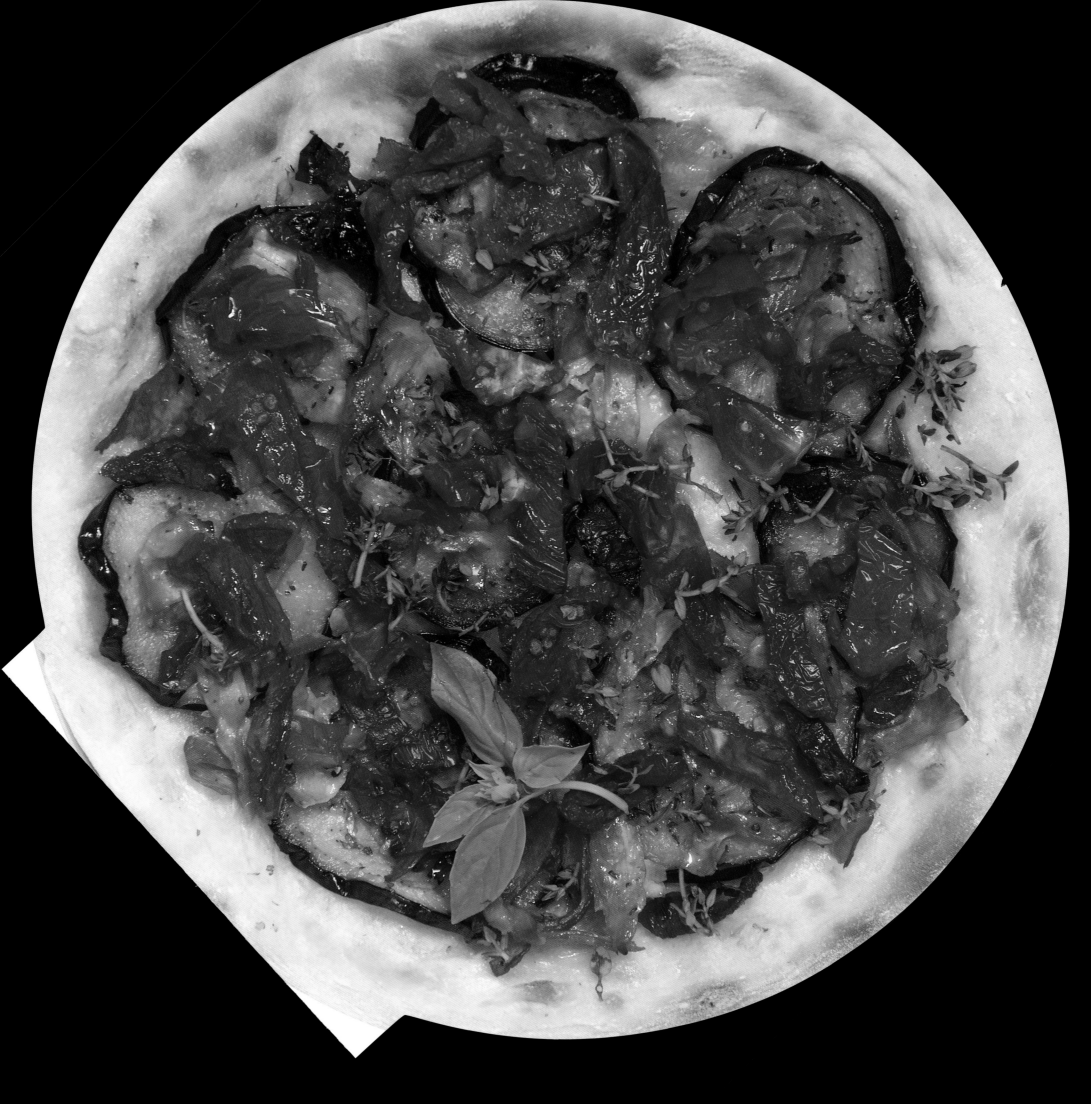

pizza with ham & mushrooms

CRUST

Basic pizza dough (see pages 8–11)

TOPPING

1 cup (250 g) diced canned tomatoes, with juice • 3 ounces (90 g) ham, thinly sliced and chopped • 12–15 mixed mushrooms preserved in oil
4 ounces (120 g) mozzarella cheese, thinly sliced or shredded
Salt and freshly ground black pepper • 1 tablespoon extra-virgin olive oil

SERVES 2 • PREPARATION 15 MINUTES + TIME TO PREPARE THE DOUGH & LET RISE
COOKING 10–15 MINUTES

CRUST **1. Prepare** the pizza dough following the instructions on pages 8–11. Set aside to rise. **2. Preheat** the oven to 500°F (250°C/gas 10). **3. Oil** a 12-inch (30-cm) pizza pan. **4. Knead** the risen pizza dough briefly on a lightly floured work surface, then press it into the prepared pan using your hands. TOPPING **5. Spread** the dough evenly with the tomatoes, ham, and mushrooms, leaving a 1/2-inch (1-cm) border all around. Top with the mozzarella and season with salt and pepper. Drizzle with the oil. **6. Bake** for 10–15 minutes, until the crust is crisp and golden brown and the cheese is bubbling and beginning to brown. **7. Serve** hot.

Ham and mushrooms are a classic pizza combination.

● If you liked this recipe, try the ham pizza on page 38.

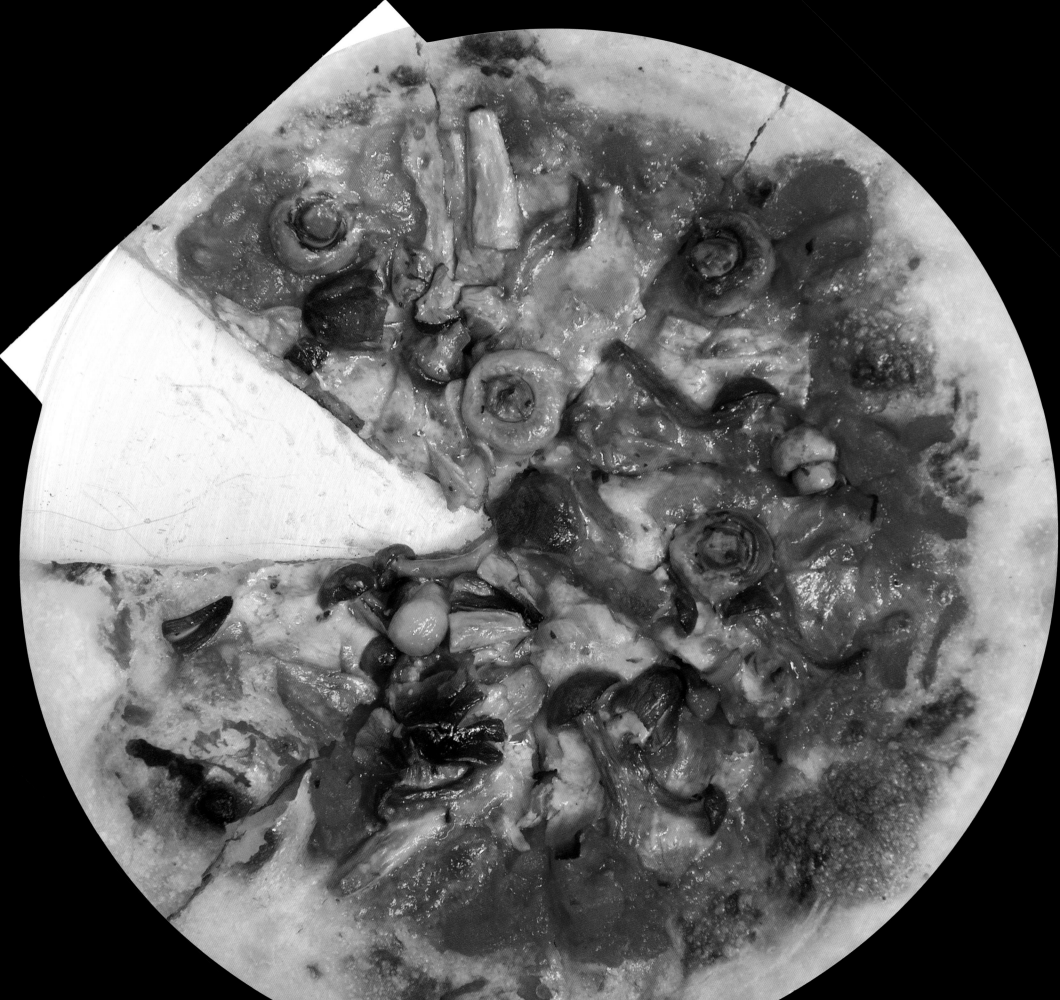

pizza with beef, zucchini & eggplant

CRUST

Basic pizza dough (see pages 8–11)

TOPPING

2 small zucchini (courgettes), thinly sliced • Salt • 6 tablespoons (90 ml) extra-virgin olive oil • 1 small eggplant (aubergine), thinly sliced lengthwise • 1 small onion, very finely chopped • 1 clove garlic, very finely chopped • 1 small carrot, very finely chopped • 1 stalk celery, very finely chopped • 8 ounces (250 g) ground (minced) beef • ¼ cup (60 ml) dry white wine • ⅓ cup (90 ml) beef stock • 2 tablespoons tomato paste (concentrate) • Freshly ground black pepper

SERVES 2 • PREPARATION 30 MINUTES + TIME TO PREPARE THE DOUGH & LET RISE
COOKING 2 HOURS 25–30 MINUTES

CRUST 1. Prepare the pizza dough following the instructions on pages 8–11. Set aside to rise. **TOPPING 2. Put** the zucchini and eggplant in a colander and sprinkle with salt. Let drain for 1 hour. **3. Heat** 2 tablespoons of oil in a medium saucepan over medium heat. Add the onion, garlic, carrot, and celery and sauté until tender, about 5 minutes. Add the beef and sauté until browned, about 5 minutes. Add the wine and simmer until it evaporates, about 2 minutes. Stir in the stock and tomato paste. Season with pepper.

Cover and simmer over low heat for 2 hours. **4. Preheat** the oven to 500°F (250°C/gas 10). **5. Oil** a 12-inch (30-cm) pizza pan. **6. Heat** the remaining 4 tablespoons oil in a large frying pan over medium heat. Fry the zucchini and eggplant in batches until tender, about 5 minutes per batch. **7. Knead** the risen pizza dough briefly on a lightly floured work surface, then press it into the prepared pan using your hands. **8. Arrange** the zucchini and eggplant on top. Cover with the meat sauce. **9. Bake** for 10–15 minutes, until the crust is crisp and golden brown. **10. Serve** hot.

The rich topping on this pizza needs a thick crust; be sure to use the thicker crust option on page 8.

• *If you liked this recipe, try the pizza with ground beef & onions on page 78.*

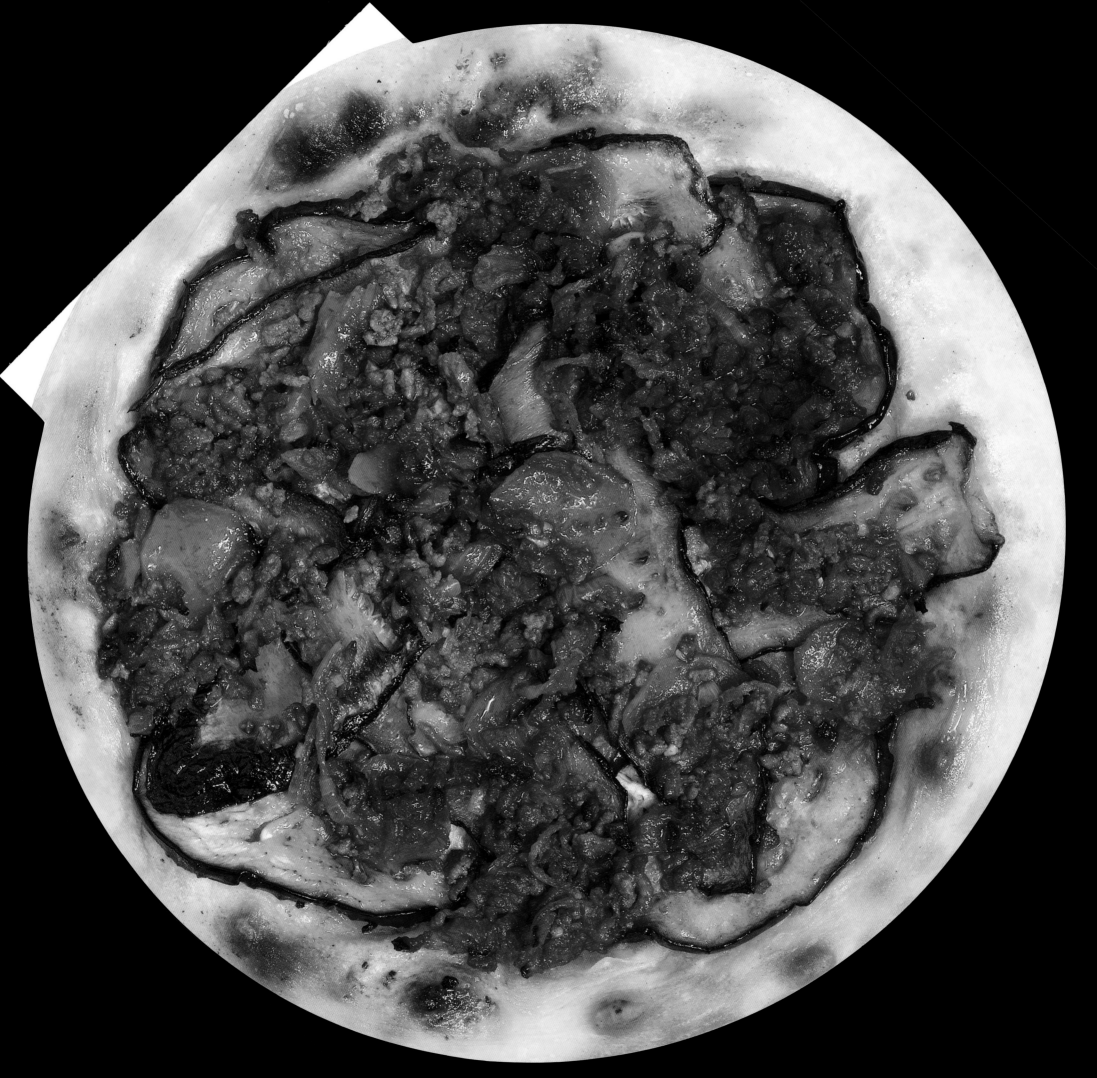

cheese pizza with **ham & mushrooms**

CRUST

Basic pizza dough (see pages 8–11)

TOPPING

1 cup (250 g) diced canned tomatoes, with juice • Salt and freshly ground black pepper • 1/4 cup (60 ml) extra-virgin olive oil • 8 ounces (250 g) white mushrooms, sliced • 1 clove garlic, lightly crushed but whole • 4 ounces (120 g) ham, chopped • 4 ounces (120 g) mozzarella cheese, thinly sliced or shredded 3 ounces (90 g) Gorgonzola cheese, cut into small cubes • 1/2 teaspoon dried oregano

SERVES 2 • PREPARATION 25 MINUTES + TIME TO PREPARE THE DOUGH & LET RISE
COOKING 20–25 MINUTES

CRUST 1. Prepare the pizza dough following the instructions on pages 8–11. Set aside to rise. **2. Preheat** the oven to 500°F (250°C/gas 10). **3. Oil** a 12-inch (30-cm) pizza pan. TOPPING **4. Place** the tomatoes in a small bowl and season with salt and pepper. Add 2 tablespoons of oil and mix well. **5. Heat** the remaining 2 tablespoons oil in a large frying pan over medium heat. Add the mushrooms and garlic and sauté until tender and most of the cooking juices have evaporated, 6–8

minutes. Remove from the heat. Discard the garlic. **6. Knead** the risen pizza dough briefly on a lightly floured work surface, then press it into the prepared pan using your hands. Spread the dough evenly with the tomato mixture, leaving a 1/2-inch (1-cm) border all around. **7. Spread** the ham, mushroom mixture, mozzarella, and Gorgonzola. **8. Bake** for 10–15 minutes, until the crust is crisp and golden brown and the cheeses are bubbling. **9. Sprinkle** with oregano. **10. Serve** hot.

• If you liked this recipe, try the pizza with ham & mushrooms on page 84.

whole-wheat pizza with 3-cheese topping

CRUST

Whole-wheat (wholemeal) pizza dough (see page 12)

TOPPING

1 tablespoon extra-virgin olive oil · 2 tablespoons milk · 2 ounces (60 g) Fontina or other mild firm cheese, thinly sliced · 2 ounces (60 g) Gorgonzola cheese, thinly sliced 2 ounces (60 g) mozzarella cheese, thinly sliced or shredded · Salt and freshly ground black pepper · 1 tablespoon finely chopped fresh oregano

SERVES 2 · PREPARATION 15 MINUTES + TIME TO PREPARE THE DOUGH & LET RISE · COOKING 10–15 MINUTES

CRUST **1. Prepare** the whole-wheat pizza dough following the instructions on page 12. Set aside to rise for 2 hours. **2. Oil** a 12-inch (30-cm) pizza pan. **3. Knead** the risen pizza dough briefly on a lightly floured work surface, then press it into the prepared pan using your hands. Let rise for another 30 minutes. **4. Preheat** the oven to 500°F (250°C/gas 10). TOPPING **5. Beat** the oil and milk in a small bowl. Brush the dough evenly with this mixture, leaving a ½-inch (1-cm) border all around. Top with alternate layers of the three cheeses. Season with pepper. **6. Bake** for 10–15 minutes, until the crust is crisp and golden brown and the cheeses are bubbling and beginning to brown. **7. Sprinkle** with the oregano. **8. Serve** hot.

In Italy fresh mozzarella cheese is used to top pizzas. In the United States there are now many different kinds of mozzarella available, most of which is dried and melts beautifully over pizza.

● If you liked this recipe, try the pizza bianca on page 30.

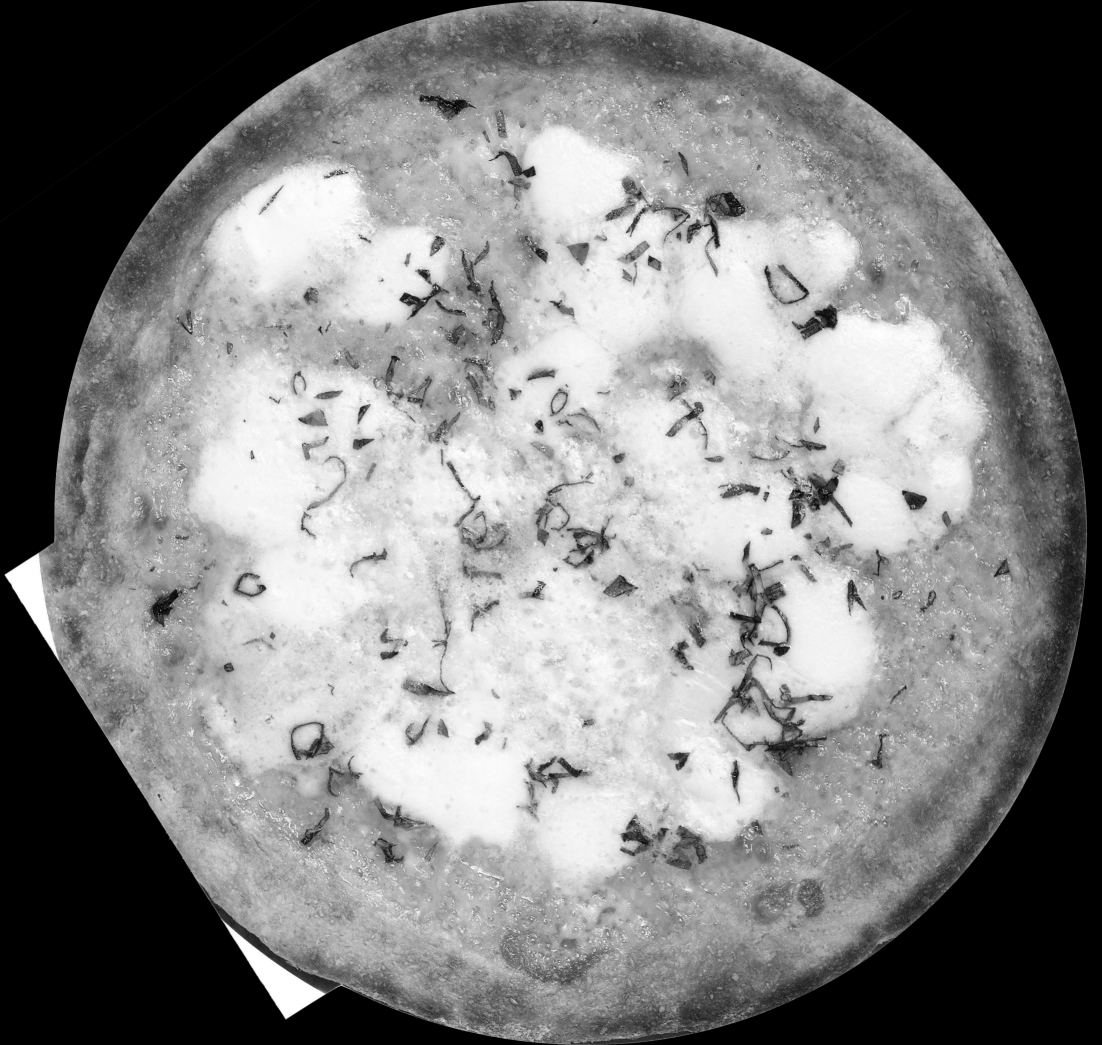

pancetta & potato
pizza

SERVES 2 · PREPARATION 15 MINUTES + TIME TO PREPARE THE DOUGH & LET RISE

COOKING 30–40 MINUTES

CRUST

Basic pizza dough (see pages 8–11)

TOPPING

⅓ cup (90 ml) extra-virgin olive oil · Sprig of rosemary
Sprig of thyme · 12 ounces (350 g) potatoes, peeled and cut into small cubes
Salt · 4 ounces (120 g) mozzarella cheese, thinly sliced or shredded
2 ounces (60 g) pancetta, sliced

CRUST **1. Prepare** the pizza dough following the instructions on pages 8–11. Set aside to rise. **2. Preheat** the oven to 400°F (200°C/gas 8). **3. Oil** a 12-inch (30-cm) pizza pan. TOPPING **4. Heat** the oil in a roasting pan over medium heat. Add the rosemary, thyme, and potatoes. Season with salt and mix well to coat. Bake until the potatoes are almost tender and beginning to brown, 20–25 minutes.

5. Increase the oven temperature to 500°F (250°C/gas 10.) **6. Knead** the risen pizza dough briefly on a lightly floured work surface, then press it into the prepared pan using your hands. **7. Cover** with the mozzarella and top with the pancetta and potatoes, leaving a ½-inch (1-cm) border all around. **8. Bake** for 10–15 minutes, until the crust and potatoes are crisp and golden brown. **9. Serve** hot.

Serve this pizza with a mixed green salad for a nutritious and complete meal. If you can't get good quality pancetta, replace with the same quantity of bacon.

● If you liked this recipe, try the pizza with artichokes & pancetta on page 74.

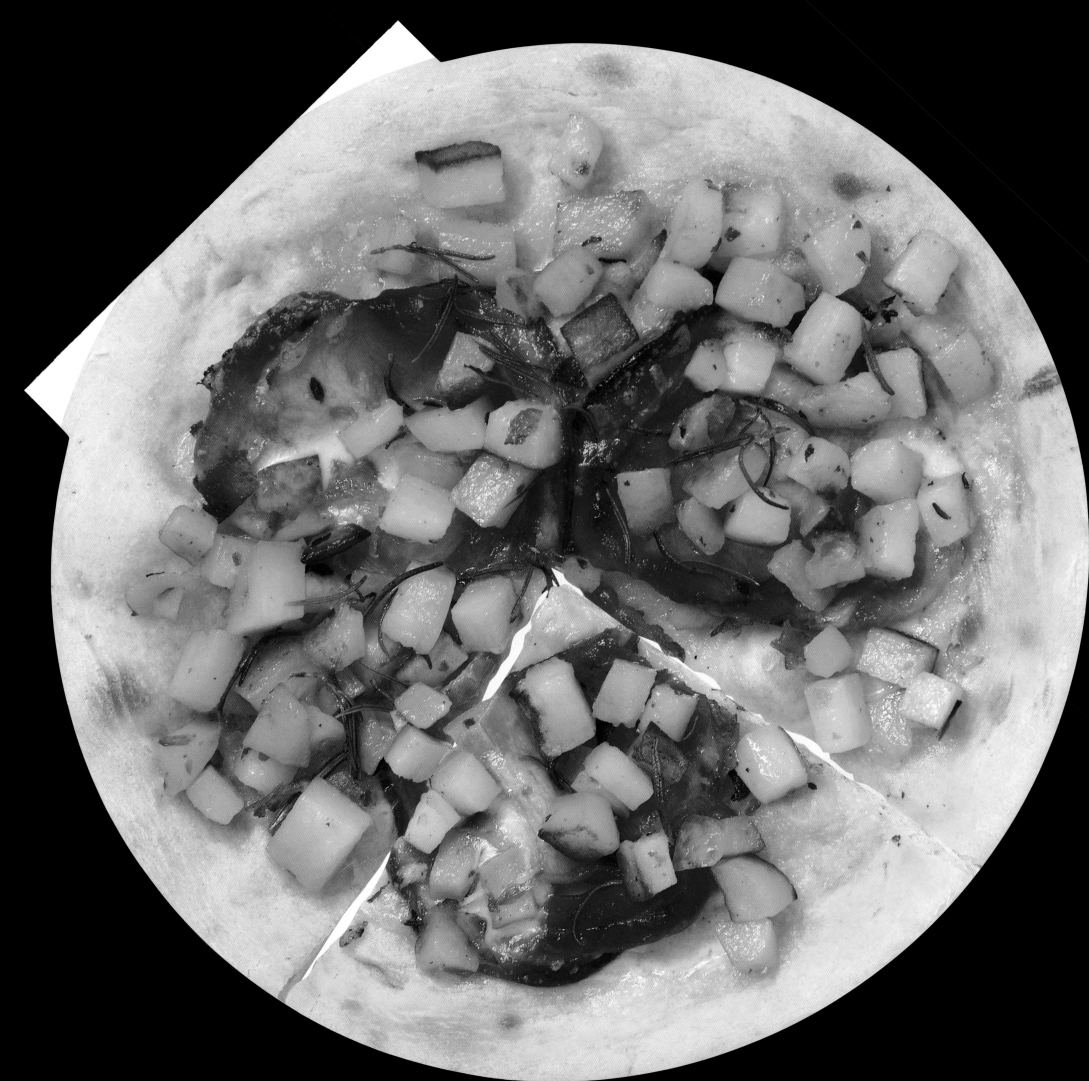

Mediterranean pizza

CRUST

Basic pizza dough (see pages 8–11)

TOPPING

3 medium-large tomatoes · Salt · 1 tablespoon extra-virgin olive oil
1 clove garlic, finely chopped · 5 ounces (150 g) tuna in oil, drained and broken into
chunks · 6 anchovy fillets · 8–10 large black olives · 1/2 teaspoon dried oregano
1 tablespoon capers in brine, drained

SERVES 2 · PREPARATION 15 MINUTES + TIME TO PREPARE THE DOUGH & LET RISE
COOKING 15–20 MINUTES

CRUST **1. Prepare** the pizza dough following the instructions on pages 8–11. Set aside to rise. **TOPPING** **2. Blanch** the tomatoes in boiling water for 30 seconds, then slip off the skins. Cut in half and squeeze gently to remove the seeds. Chop coarsely then set aside in a colander. Sprinkle lightly with salt and let drain for 10 minutes. **3. Heat** the oil and garlic in a small frying pan over medium heat. Add the tomatoes and sauté for 4–5 minutes. Set aside. **4. Preheat** the oven to 500°F (250°C/gas 10.) **5. Oil** a 12-inch (30-cm) pizza pan. **6. Knead** the risen pizza dough briefly on a lightly floured work surface, then press it into the prepared pan using your hands. **7. Spread** the tomato mixture evenly over the dough, leaving a 1/2-inch (1-cm) border all around. Top with the tuna, anchovies, olives, oregano, and capers. **8. Bake** for 10–15 minutes, until the crust is crisp and golden brown. **9. Serve** hot.

With tomatoes, tuna, olives, capers, and oregano, this pizza has all the flavors of the Mediterranean.

● If you liked this recipe, try the Sicilian pizza on page 52.

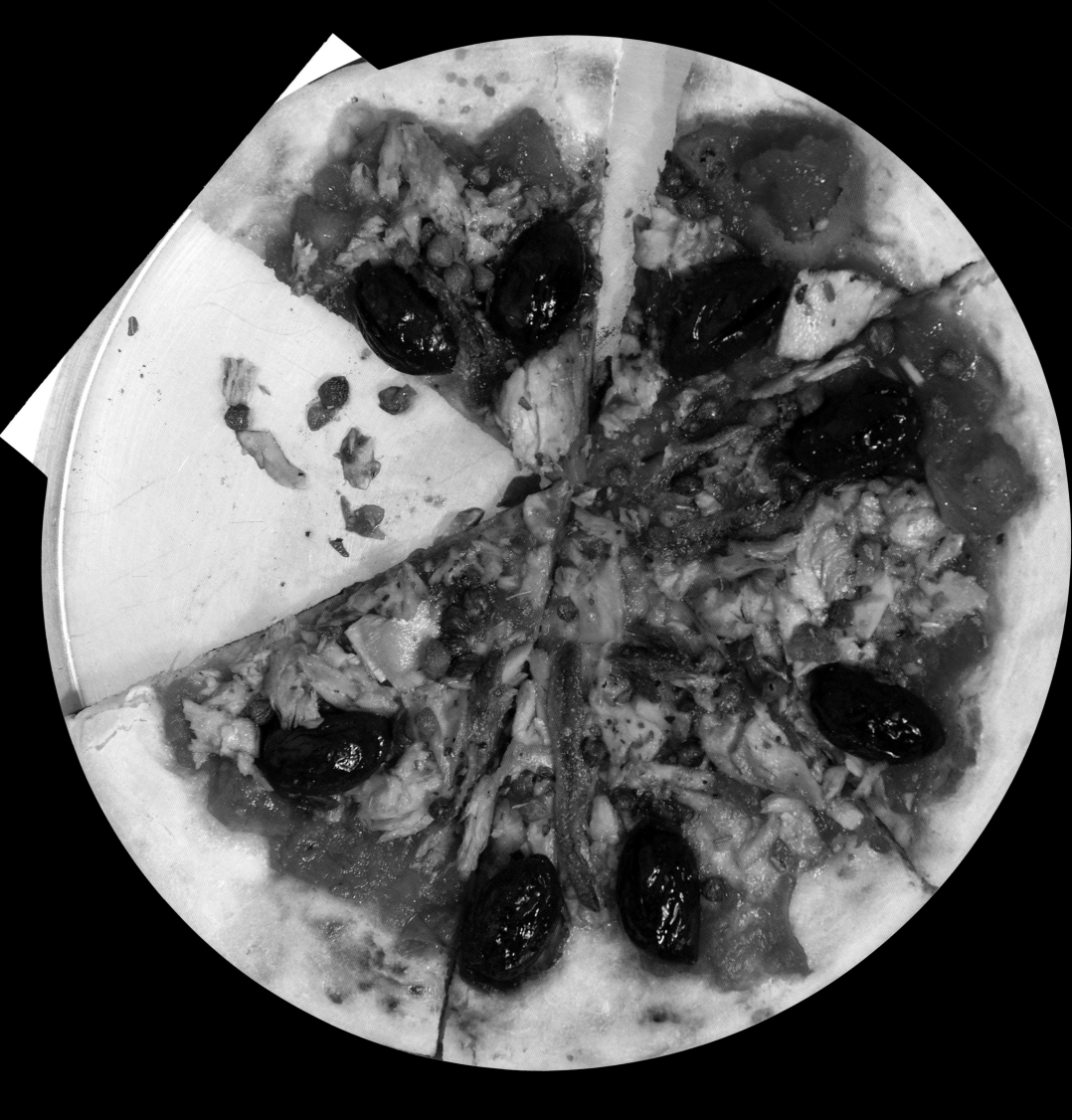

CRUST
Whole-wheat pizza (wholemeal) dough
(see page 12)

TOPPING
3 tablespoons extra-virgin olive oil · 1 small eggplant (aubergine), with skin, cut in small cubes · 1 zucchini (courgette), cut in small cubes · 1 clove garlic, finely chopped · 1 tablespoon finely chopped fresh parsley · 10–12 green olives, pitted · 3½ ounces (100 g) pecorino cheese, coarsely grated · 4–6 cherry tomatoes, halved

SERVES 2 · PREPARATION 20 MINUTES + TIME TO PREPARE THE DOUGH & LET RISE
COOKING 15–20 MINUTES

whole-wheat pizza
with **vegetable topping**

96

CRUST **1. Prepare** the whole-wheat pizza dough following the instructions on page 12. Set aside to rise for 2 hours. **2. Preheat** the oven to 500°F (250°C/gas 10). **3. Oil** a 12-inch (30-cm) pizza pan.

TOPPING **4. Heat** the oil in a medium frying pan over medium heat. Add the eggplant, zucchini, garlic, and parsley and sauté until the vegetables are beginning to soften, about 5 minutes.

5. Knead the risen pizza dough briefly on a lightly floured work surface, then press it into the prepared pan using your hands. **6. Spread** with the vegetable mixture, olives, pecorino, and cherry tomatoes, leaving a ½-inch (1-cm) border all around. **7. Bake** for 10–15 minutes, until the crust is crisp and golden brown and the cheese is bubbling and beginning to brown. **8. Serve** hot.

For extra taste and color, add 2–3 tablespoons of frozen peas and a small carrot, cut into small cubes. Sauté with the eggplant and zucchini.

● If you liked this recipe, try the bell pepper pizza on page 58.

Calabrian pizza
with **ricotta & sausage**

CRUST

Basic pizza dough (see pages 8–11)

TOPPING

1 cup (250 g) very fresh ricotta cheese, well drained · 5 ounces (150 g) Italian sausages, peeled and crumbled · 1/2 cup (60 g) freshly grated pecorino cheese · 1–2 hard-boiled eggs, peeled and thickly sliced

Salt and freshly ground black pepper

SERVES 2 · PREPARATION 15 MINUTES + TIME TO PREPARE THE DOUGH & LET RISE

COOKING 10–15 MINUTES

Calabrian sausage is made with pork and sweet peppers or spicy chiles, often with wild fennel seeds added, too. It is very flavorful. Substitute a well-spiced local sausage if you can't find it.

CRUST **1. Prepare** the pizza dough following the instructions on pages 8–11. Set aside to rise. **2. Preheat** the oven to 500°F (250°C/gas 10). **3. Oil** a 12-inch (30-cm) pizza pan. **4. Knead** the risen pizza dough briefly on a lightly floured work surface, then press it into the prepared pan using your hands. TOPPING **5. Spread** the dough evenly with the ricotta, sausages, and pecorino, leaving a 1/2-inch (1-cm) border all around. Top with slices of boiled egg. Season with salt and pepper. **6. Bake** for 10–15 minutes, until the crust is crisp and golden brown. **7. Serve** hot.

98

• If you liked this recipe, try the Palermo-style pizza on page 50.

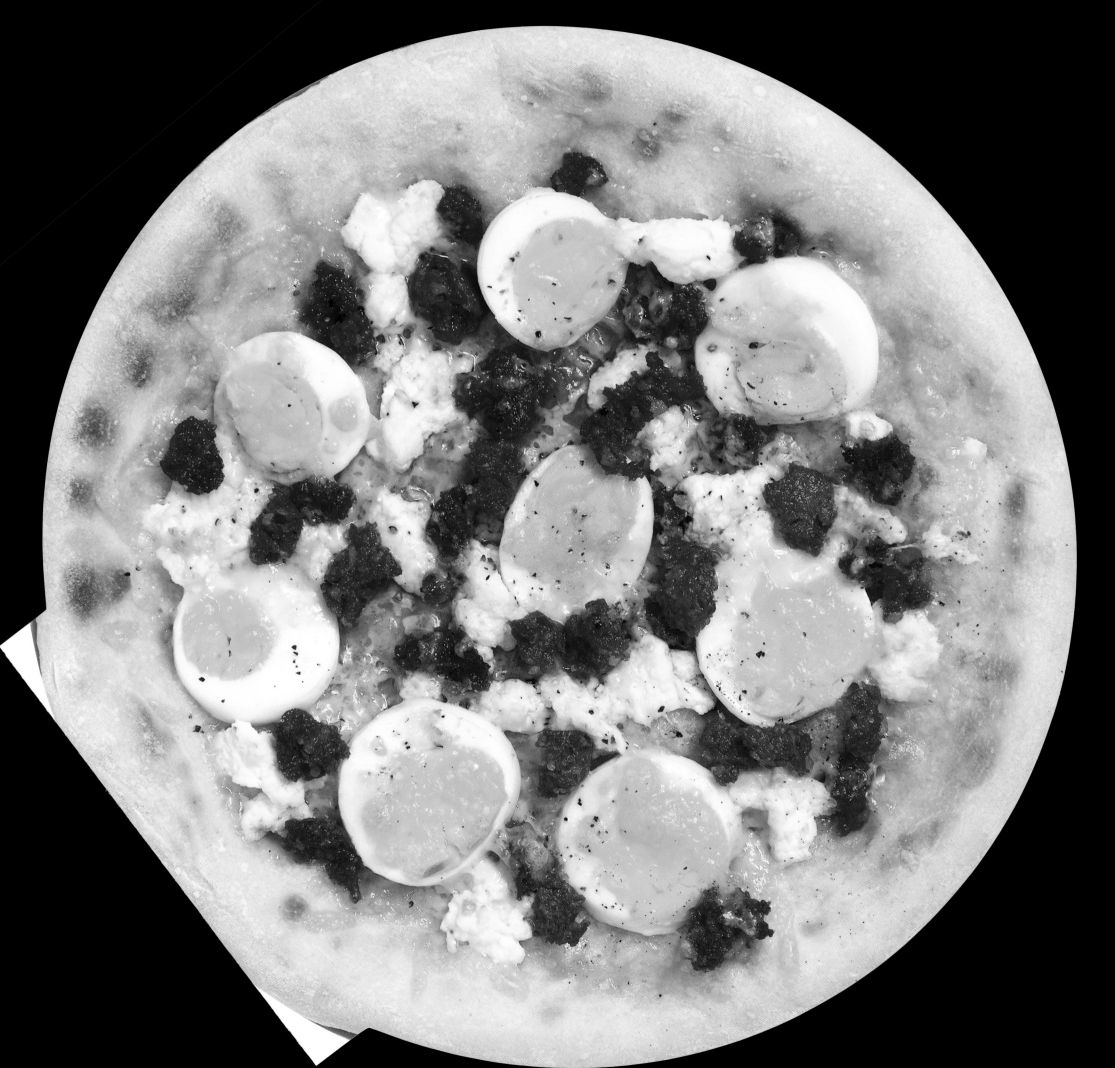

Greek pizza

CRUST

Basic pizza dough (see pages 8–11)

TOPPING

1 cup (250 g) diced canned tomatoes, with juice • 1 medium tomato, thinly sliced • 2 cloves garlic, thinly sliced • 1 small red onion, thinly sliced
4 ounces (120 g) feta cheese, crumbled • 8–10 Kalamata olives
1 tablespoon extra-virgin olive oil

SERVES 2 • **PREPARATION** 15 MINUTES + TIME TO PREPARE THE DOUGH & LET RISE
COOKING 10–15 MINUTES

CRUST **1. Prepare** the pizza dough following the instructions on pages 8–11. Set aside to rise. **2. Preheat** the oven to 500°F (250°C/gas 10). **3. Oil** a 12-inch (30-cm) pizza pan. **4. Knead** the risen pizza dough briefly on a lightly floured work surface, then press it into the prepared pan using your hands.
TOPPING **5. Spread** the dough evenly with the tomatoes, leaving a ½-inch (1-cm) border all around. Top with the slices of tomato, garlic, onion, feta, and olives. Sprinkle with the cheese and drizzle with the oil. **6. Bake** for 10–15 minutes, until the crust is crisp and golden brown. **7. Serve** hot.

● If you liked this recipe, try the Sardinian pizza on page 48.

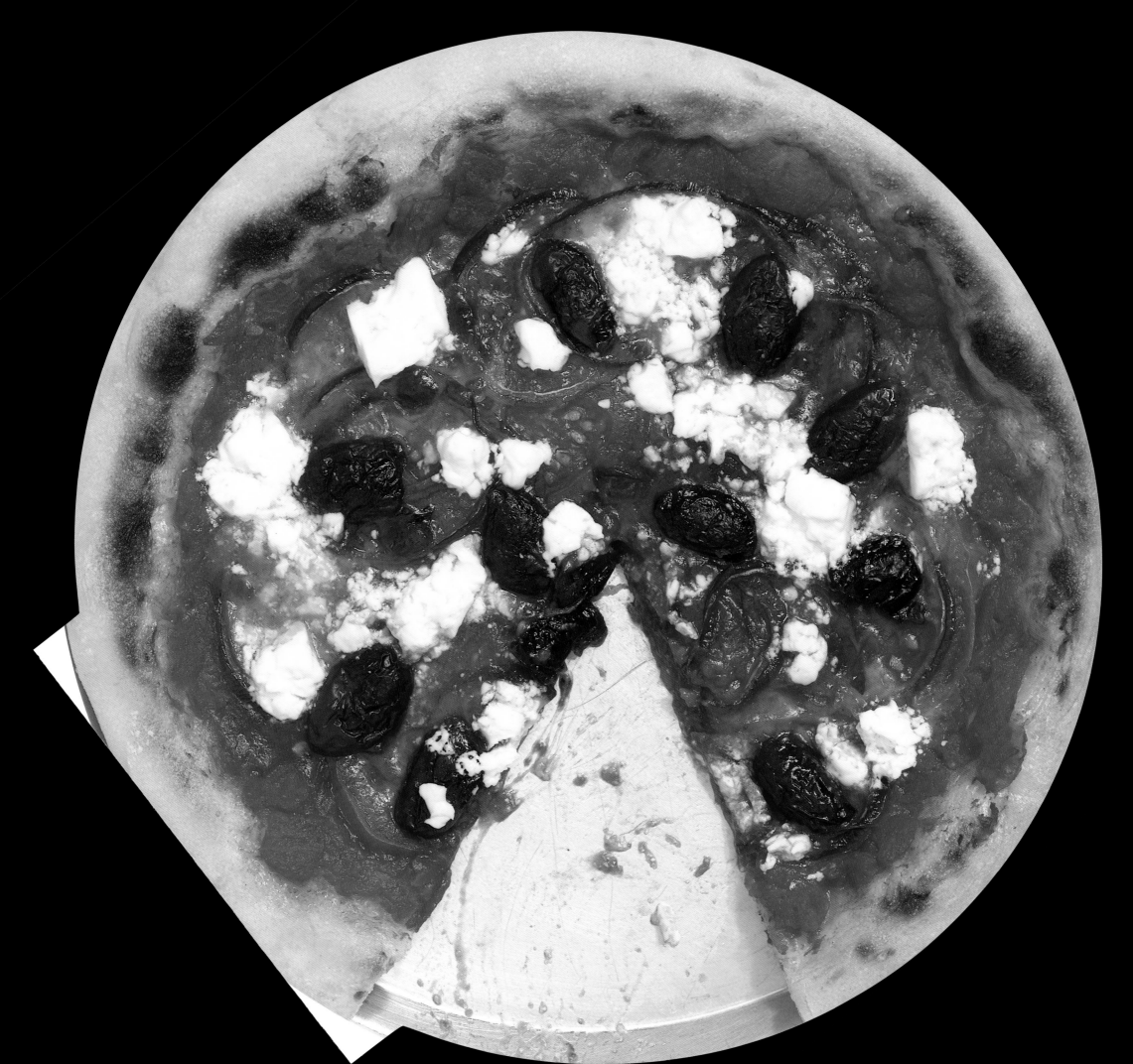

pizza with 4 cheeses & pesto

CRUST

Basic pizza dough (see pages 8–11)

TOPPING

3 ounces (90 g) mozzarella cheese, thinly sliced or shredded · 2 ounces (60 g) coarsely grated provolone cheese · 2 ounces (60 g) Gorgonzola cheese, crumbled · 3 tablespoons coarsely grated pecorino cheese · 1 recipe pesto (see page 24)

SERVES 2 · **PREPARATION** 15 MINUTES + TIME TO PREPARE THE DOUGH & LET RISE · **COOKING** 10–15 MINUTES

CRUST **1. Prepare** the pizza dough following the instructions on pages 8–11. Set aside to rise. **2. Preheat** the oven to 500°F (250°C/gas 10). **3. Oil** a 12-inch (30-cm) pizza pan. **4. Knead** the risen pizza dough briefly on a lightly floured work surface, then press it into the prepared pan using your hands. **TOPPING 5. Spread** the dough evenly with the four cheeses, leaving a ½-inch (1-cm) border all around. **6. Bake** for 10–15 minutes, until the crust is crisp and golden brown and the cheeses are bubbling and beginning to brown. **7. Top** with the pesto. **8. Serve** hot.

Provolone cheese can be either sweet or spicy, plain or smoked. Use a spicy, aged provolone for best results with this pizza. If preferred, substitute a tasty, semi-hard local cheese.

● **If you liked this recipe, try the two-cheese pizza on page 54.**

102

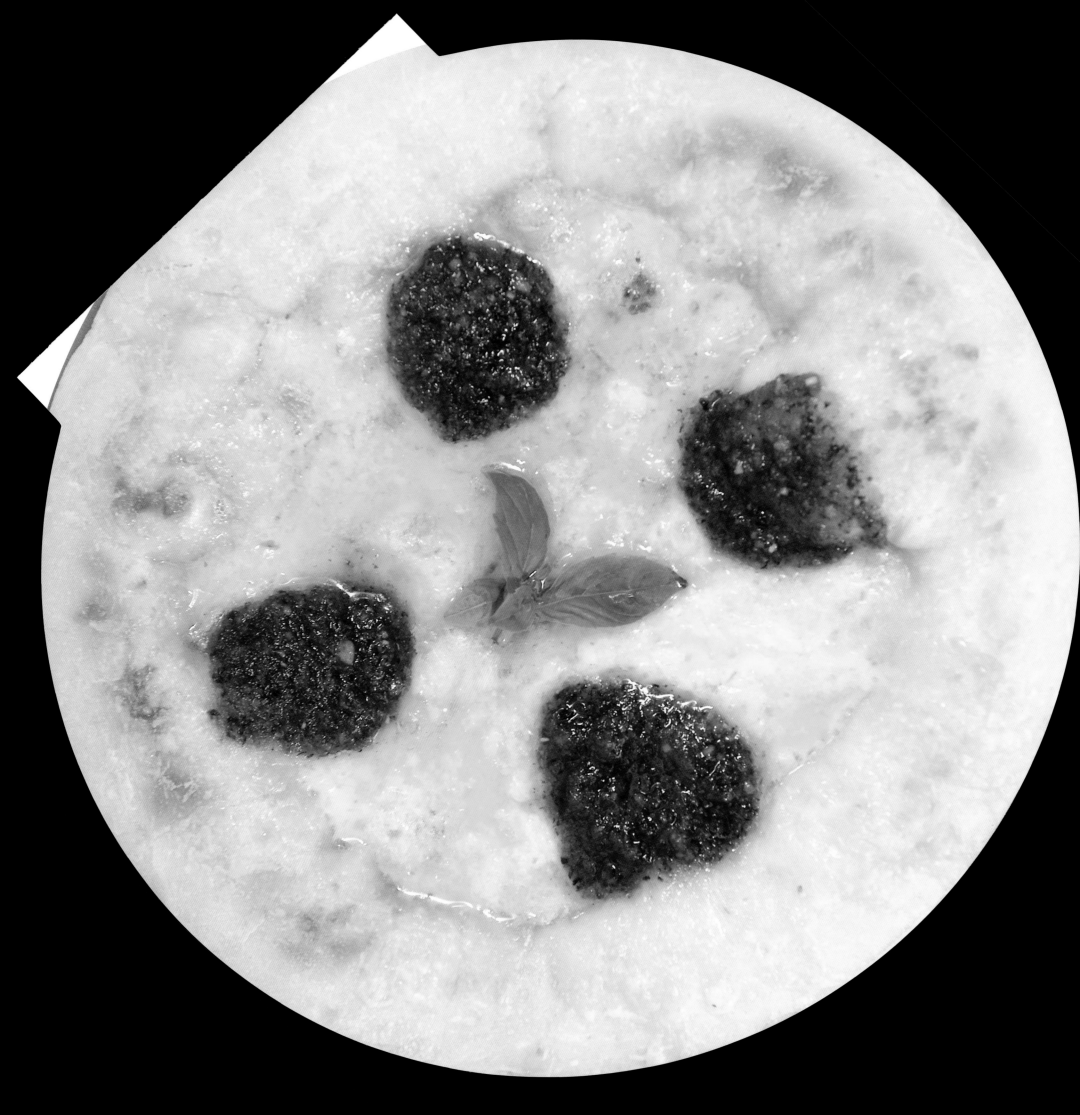

CRUST

Basic pizza dough (see pages 8–11)

TOPPING

2 tablespoons extra-virgin olive oil · 1 small onion, finely chopped · 2 cloves garlic, finely chopped · 2 small white mushrooms, sliced · 1 tablespoon tomato paste (concentrate) · 1 cup (250 g) diced canned tomatoes, with juice ½ teaspoon dried oregano · ¼ teaspoon fennel seeds, crushed · 3 ounces (90 g) pepperoni (salami), thinly sliced · 4 ounces (120 g) mozzarella cheese, thinly sliced or shredded · 2 tablespoons freshly grated Parmesan cheese

SERVES 2 · PREPARATION 15 MINUTES + TIME TO PREPARE THE DOUGH & LET RISE
COOKING 25–30 MINUTES

pizza with pepperoni, mushrooms & fennel

CRUST **1. Prepare** the pizza dough following the instructions on pages 8–11. Set aside to rise. **2. Preheat** the oven to 500°F (250°C/gas 10). **3. Oil** a 12-inch (30-cm) pizza pan. **4. Knead** the risen pizza dough briefly on a lightly floured work surface, then press it into the prepared pan using your hands. TOPPING **5. Heat** 1 tablespoon of oil in a small pan and sauté the onion until softened, 3–4 minutes. Remove from the pan and set aside. Heat the remaining 1 tablespoon of oil in the same pan.

Add the garlic and mushrooms and sauté until softened, 3–4 minutes. Add the tomato paste, tomatoes, oregano, and fennel seeds and simmer for 5 minutes. **6. Spread** the tomato mixture evenly over the dough, leaving a ½-inch (1-cm) border all around. Top with the pepperoni, onion, mozzarella, and Parmesan. **7. Bake** for 10–15 minutes, until the crust is crisp and golden brown and the cheeses are bubbling and beginning to brown. **8. Serve** hot.

This pizza has a thick, nutritious topping that will go best with a thick crust (see page 8).

• If you liked this recipe, try the pizza with spicy salami on page 70.

tomato, garlic & sausage

pizza with

CRUST

Basic pizza dough (see pages 8–11)

TOPPING

1 tablespoon extra-virgin olive oil • 8 ounces (250 g) spicy Italian sausage, casing removed and crumbled • 2 cloves garlic, thinly sliced • 1 cup (250 g) diced canned tomatoes, with juice • 4 ounces (120 g) mozzarella cheese, thinly sliced or shredded ½ teaspoon dried oregano • Salt and freshly ground black pepper

Fresh basil, to garnish

SERVES 2 • **PREPARATION** 15 MINUTES + TIME TO PREPARE THE DOUGH & LET RISE

COOKING 15–20 MINUTES

CRUST 1. Prepare the pizza dough following the instructions on pages 8–11. Set aside to rise. **2. Preheat** the oven to 500°F (250°C/gas 10). **3. Oil** a 12-inch (30-cm) pizza pan. **4. Knead** the risen pizza dough briefly on a lightly floured work surface, then press it into the prepared pan using your hands. **TOPPING 5. Heat** the oil in a small pan over medium heat. Add the sausage and garlic and sauté until browned, about 5 minutes. Drain off the fat and set aside. **6. Spread** the dough evenly with the tomatoes, leaving a ½-inch (1-cm) border all around. Top with the sausage mixture and mozzarella. Season with the oregano, salt, and pepper. **7. Bake** for 10–15 minutes, until the crust is crisp and golden brown and the cheese is bubbling and beginning to brown. **8. Garnish** with the basil. **9. Serve** hot.

This is another hearty pizza that goes best with a thick crust (see page 8).

● If you liked this recipe, try the pizza with sausage & mushrooms on page 66.

whole-wheat pizza with cheese, herbs & tomatoes

CRUST
Whole-wheat pizza (wholemeal) dough (see page 12)

TOPPING
1 cup (250 g) diced canned tomatoes, with juice, chopped • 2 tablespoons tomato paste (concentrate) • 1 tablespoon finely chopped fresh mixed herbs (basil, thyme, parsley, oregano) • Salt and freshly ground black pepper • 1 medium ripe tomato, thinly sliced 5 ounces (150 g) freshly grated Emmental cheese • 1 tablespoon extra-virgin olive oil

SERVES 2 • PREPARATION 15 MINUTES + TIME TO PREPARE THE DOUGH & LET RISE COOKING 10–15 MINUTES

CRUST 1. Prepare the whole-wheat pizza dough following the instructions on page 12. Set aside to rise for 2 hours. **2. Preheat** the oven to 500 °F (250 °C/gas 10). **3. Oil** a 12-inch (30-cm) pizza pan. **4. Knead** the risen pizza dough briefly on a lightly floured work surface, then press it into the prepared pan using your hands. TOPPING **5. Combine** the canned tomatoes, tomato paste, and half the chopped herbs in a small bowl. Season with salt and pepper. Spread this mixture evenly over the dough, leaving a ½-inch (1-cm) border all around. Top with the sliced tomato and spread with the cheese. Drizzle with the oil. **6. Bake** for 10–15 minutes, until the dough is crisp and golden brown and the cheese is bubbling and beginning to brown. **7. Sprinkle** with the remaining herbs. **8. Serve** hot.

● **If you liked this recipe, try the four seasons pizza on page 44.**

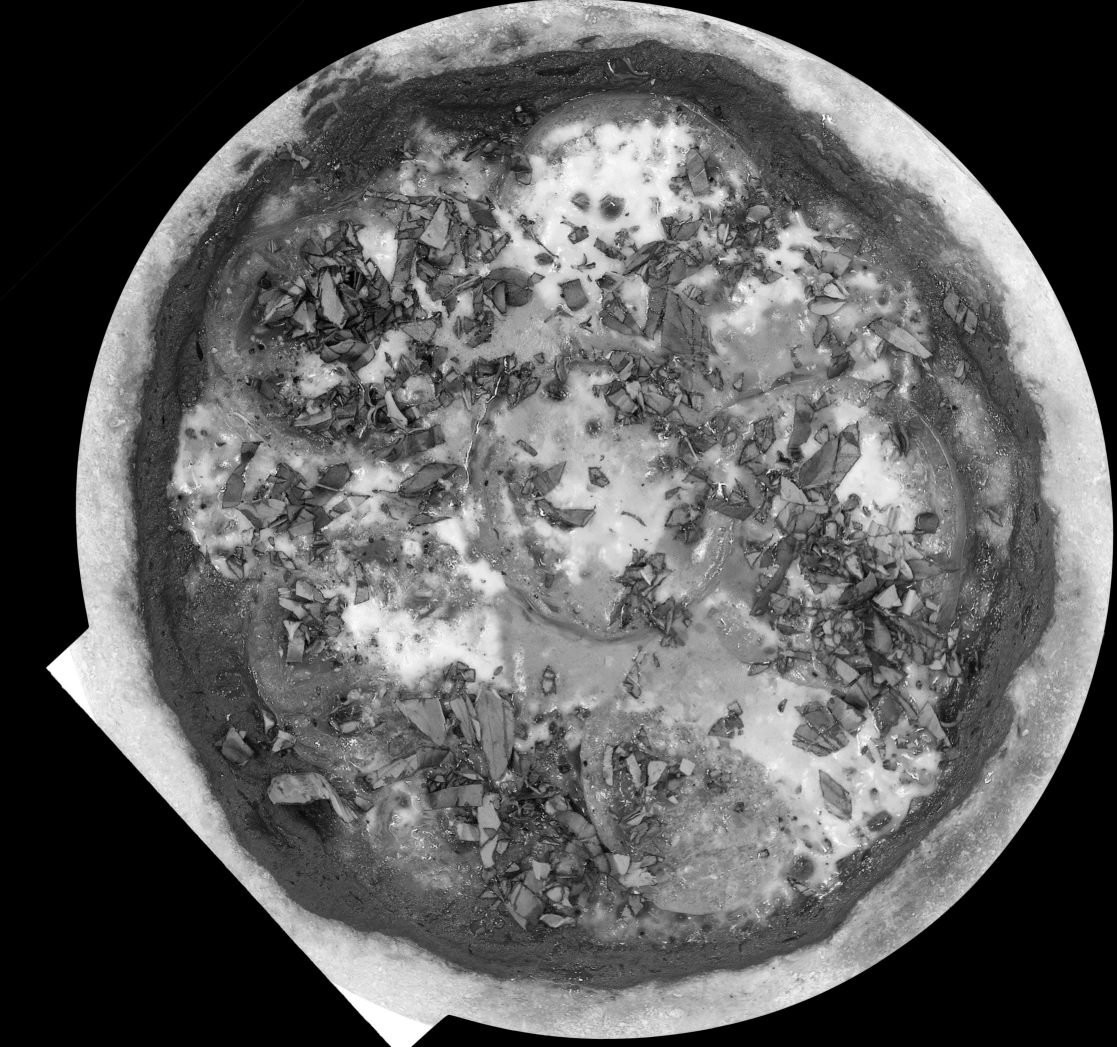

gluten-free pizza

CRUST

Gluten-free pizza dough (see page 13)

TOPPING

3–4 tablespoons tomato paste (concentrate) · 3 tablespoons freshly grated Parmesan cheese · 4 ounces (120 g) mozzarella cheese, thinly sliced or shredded 4–6 cherry tomatoes, halved · 3–4 black olives · 3–4 thin slices prosciutto (Parma ham) · ½ avocado, peeled and sliced · 1 cup (50 g) arugula (rocket) 1 tablespoon extra-virgin olive oil · 1 tablespoon balsamic vinegar

SERVES 2 · **PREPARATION** 20 MINUTES + TIME TO PREPARE THE DOUGH & LET RISE
COOKING 10–15 MINUTES

CRUST **1. Prepare** the gluten-free pizza dough following the instructions on page 13. Set aside to rise for 1 hour. **2. Preheat** the oven to 500°F (250°C/gas 10). **3. Oil** a 12-inch (30-cm) pizza pan. **4. Knead** the risen pizza dough briefly on a lightly floured work surface, then press it into the prepared pan using your hands. TOPPING **5. Spread** the dough evenly with the tomato paste, leaving a ½-inch (1-cm) border all around. Cover with the Parmesan, mozzarella, cherry tomatoes, and olives. **6. Bake** for 10–15 minutes, until the crust is crisp and golden brown and the cheese is bubbling and beginning to brown. **7. Top** with the prosciutto, avocado, and arugula. Drizzle with the oil and balsamic vinegar. **8. Serve** hot.

You can serve this topping with a plain or whole-wheat (wholemeal) pizza crust, just as you can prepare this gluten-free crust for any of the other toppings in this book.

● If you liked this recipe, try the pizza capricciosa on page 40.

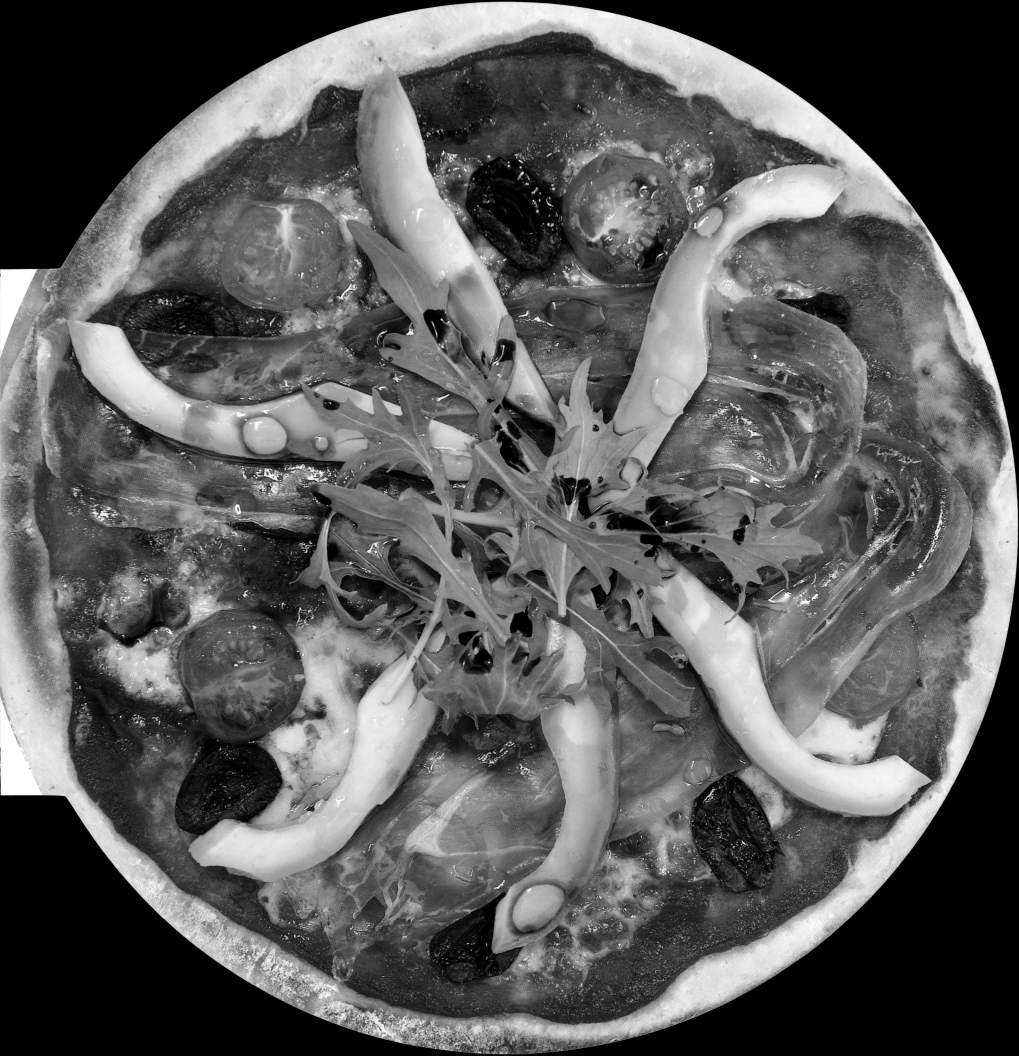

pissaladiere

CRUST

Basic pizza dough (see pages 8–11)

TOPPING

3 tablespoons extra-virgin olive oil • 2 large white onions, thinly sliced
Small handful fresh thyme leaves • 1 cup (250 g) diced canned tomatoes,
with juice • 1 (2-ounce/50-g) can or jar anchovy fillets, drained
19 black olives • Freshly ground black pepper

SERVES 2 • **PREPARATION** 20 MINUTES + TIME TO PREPARE THE DOUGH & LET RISE
COOKING 45–65 MINUTES

CRUST 1. Prepare the pizza dough following the instructions on pages 8–11. Set aside to rise. **2. Preheat** the oven to 500°F (250°C/gas 10). **3. Oil** a 12-inch (30-cm) pizza pan. **4. Knead** the risen pizza dough briefly on a lightly floured work surface, then press it into the prepared pan using your hands.

TOPPING 5. Heat the oil in a large saucepan and add the onions. Sauté until softened, about 5 minutes. Stir in the thyme, saving a little to garnish, and simmer over low heat until golden, and simmer for 20–30 minutes. Stir in the caramelized tomatoes and simmer for 10–15 minutes more. **6. Spread** the

topping evenly over the dough, leaving a ½-inch (1-cm) border all around. Arrange the anchovies over the top in a crisscross or lattice pattern. Place an olive inside each crisscross. Season generously with freshly ground black pepper. **7. Bake** for 10–15 minutes, until golden brown. **8. Sprinkle** with the remaining thyme. **9. Serve** hot.

Pissaladiere is a type of pizza made in southern France, from Marseilles to Nice, and also over the Italian border in Liguria (where it is known as *pisçaladréa*). It has a topping of sautéed (almost caramelized) onions and anchovies. Traditionally, no tomatoes were used.

● If you liked this recipe, try the pizza Napoletana on page 18.

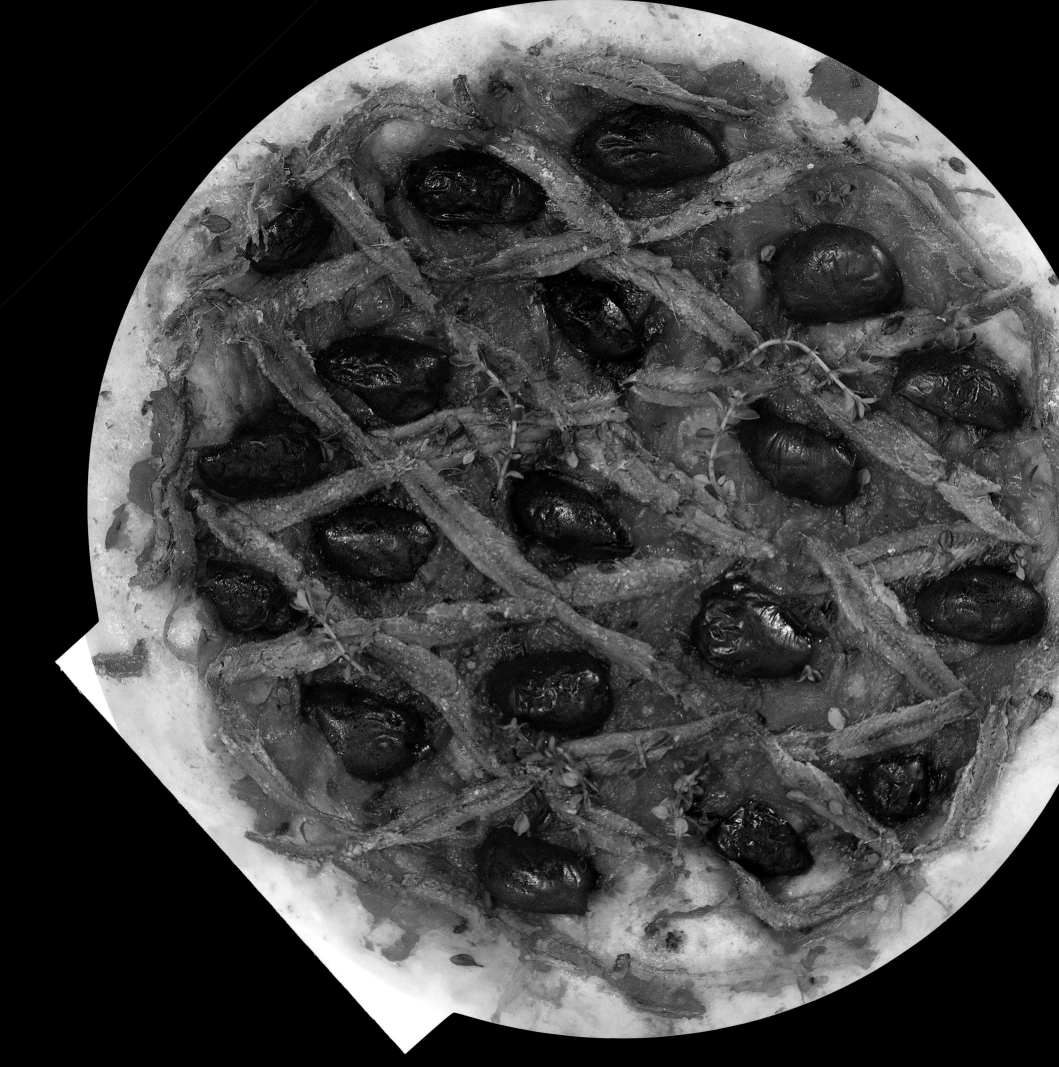

CRUST

Basic pizza dough (see pages 8–11)

TOPPING

6 ounces (200 g) Gorgonzola cheese · 1 tablespoon Worcestershire sauce1 medium white onion, very thinly sliced · ²/₃ cup (100 g) walnuts 3 ounces (90 g) cream cheese · Salt and freshly ground black pepper

SERVES 2 · **PREPARATION** 15 MINUTES + TIME TO PREPARE THE DOUGH & LET RISE
COOKING 10–15 MINUTES

pizza with
onion, cheese & walnuts

CRUST **1. Prepare** the pizza dough following the instructions on pages 8–11. Set aside to rise. **2. Preheat** the oven to 500°F (250°C/gas 10). **3. Oil** a 12-inch (30-cm) pizza pan. **4. Knead** the risen pizza dough briefly on a lightly floured work surface, then press it into the prepared pan using your hands. TOPPING **5. Mash** the Gorgonzola in small a bowl using a fork until smooth and creamy. Stir in the Worcestershire sauce.

6. Spread the dough evenly with the Gorgonzola and top with the onion, leaving a ¹/₂-inch (1-cm) border all around. Sprinkle with the walnuts. Dot with the cream cheese and season with salt and pepper. **7. Bake** for 10–15 minutes, until the crust is crisp and golden brown and the cheese is bubbling and beginning to brown. **8. Serve** hot.

● If you liked this recipe, try the cheese pizza with onion, apple & walnuts on page 26.

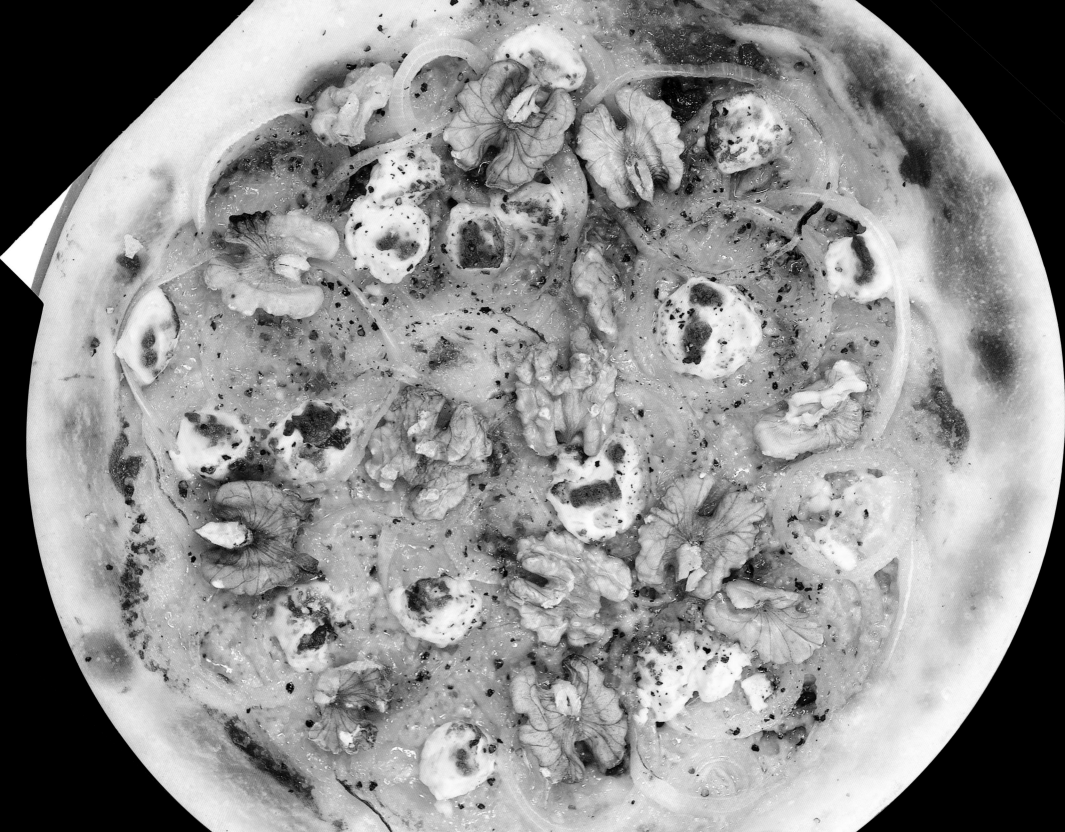

pizza with zucchini & egg

CRUST

Basic pizza dough (see pages 8–11)

TOPPING

3 tablespoons extra-virgin olive oil • 1 large onion, thinly sliced
1 zucchini (courgette), thinly sliced • Salt and freshly ground black pepper
2 tomatoes, thinly sliced • 4 ounces (120 g) mozzarella cheese,
thinly sliced or shredded • 2 eggs

SERVES 2 • **PREPARATION** 15 MINUTES + TIME TO PREPARE THE DOUGH & LET RISE

COOKING 15–25 MINUTES

CRUST **1. Prepare** the pizza dough following the instructions on pages 8–11. Set aside to rise. **2. Preheat** the oven to 500°F (250°C/gas 10). **3. Oil** a 12-inch (30-cm) pizza pan. **4. Knead** the risen pizza dough briefly on a lightly floured work surface, then press it into the prepared pan using your hands.

TOPPING **5. Heat** 2 tablespoons of oil in a large frying pan over medium heat. Add the onion and zucchini. Sauté until tender, 5–7 minutes. Season with salt and pepper. **6. Spread** the dough evenly with the tomatoes and the zucchini mixture, leaving a ½-inch (1-cm) border all around. Top with the mozzarella. Break the eggs onto the pizza. Season with salt and pepper and drizzle with the remaining 1 tablespoon of oil. **7. Bake** for 10–15 minutes, until the crust is crisp and golden brown and the eggs are cooked. **8. Serve** hot.

• If you liked this recipe, try the cheese pizza with spinach & egg on page 118.

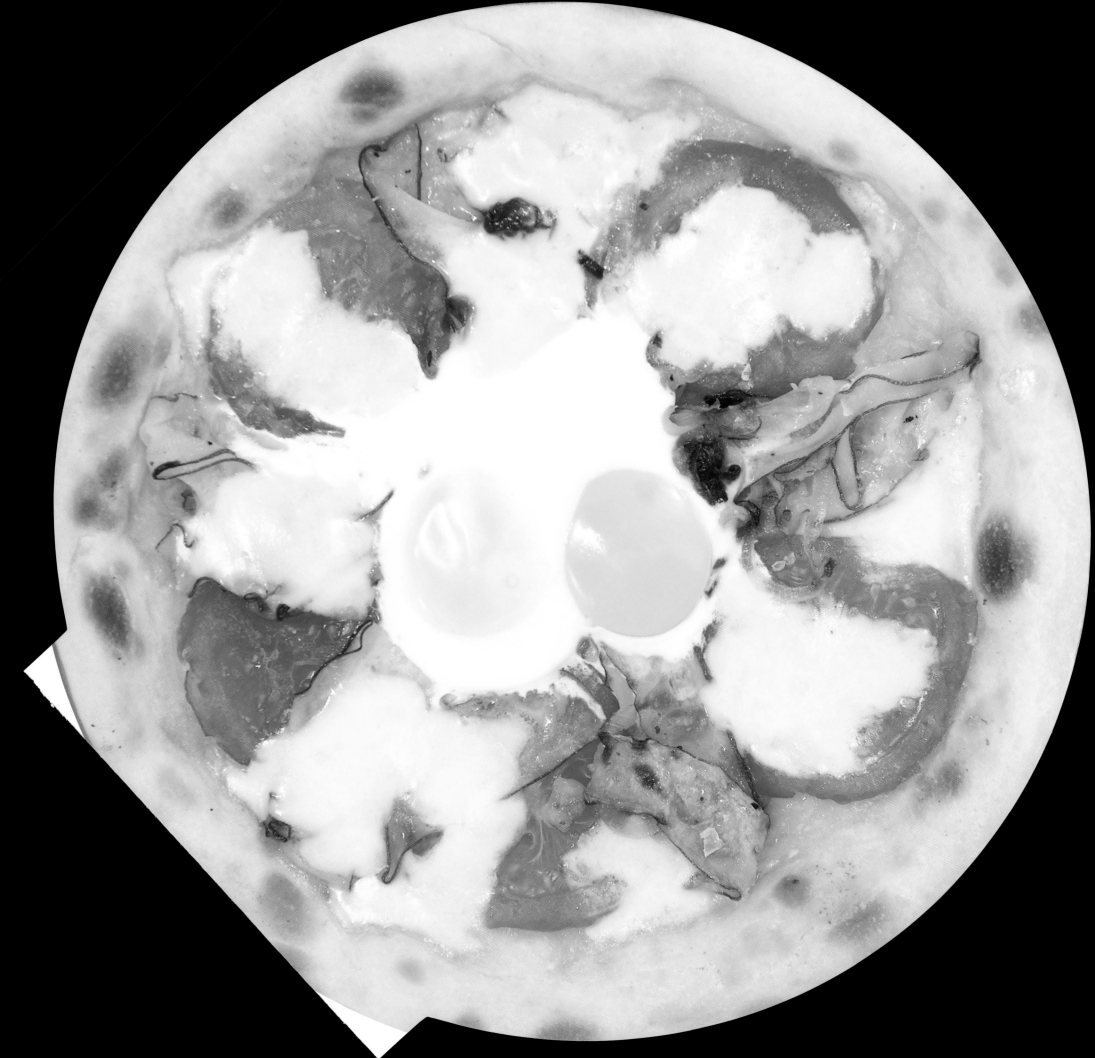

cheese pizza
with **spinach & egg**

CRUST
Basic pizza dough (see pages 8–11)

TOPPING
2 tablespoons butter · 5 ounces (150 g) cooked spinach, drained and coarsely chopped · 2 medium tomatoes, chopped · 3 ounces (90 g) thinly sliced ham, chopped 4 ounces (120 g) mozzarella cheese, thinly sliced or shredded · Salt and freshly ground black pepper · 1 egg · ½ cup (50 g) Parmesan cheese, flaked

SERVES 2 · **PREPARATION** 15 MINUTES + TIME TO PREPARE THE DOUGH & LET RISE
COOKING 15–20 MINUTES

CRUST   1. Prepare the pizza dough following the instructions on pages 8–11. Set aside to rise. **2. Preheat** the oven to 500°F (250°C/gas 10). **3. Oil** a 12-inch (30-cm) pizza pan. **4. Knead** the risen pizza dough briefly on a lightly floured work surface, then press it into the prepared pan using your hands. **TOPPING 5. Melt** the butter in a large frying pan over medium heat. Add the spinach and sauté until well mixed with the butter, 3–4 minutes. **6. Spread** the dough evenly with the chopped tomato, leaving a ½-inch (1-cm) border all around. Top with the spinach, ham, and mozzarella and break the egg into the middle. Season with salt and pepper. **7. Bake** for 10–15 minutes, until the crust is crisp and golden brown and the egg is cooked. **8. Scatter** with the Parmesan flakes. **9. Serve** hot.

This hearty pizza is perfect for brunch or a snack.

● **If you liked this recipe, try the pizza with zucchini & egg on page 116.**

118

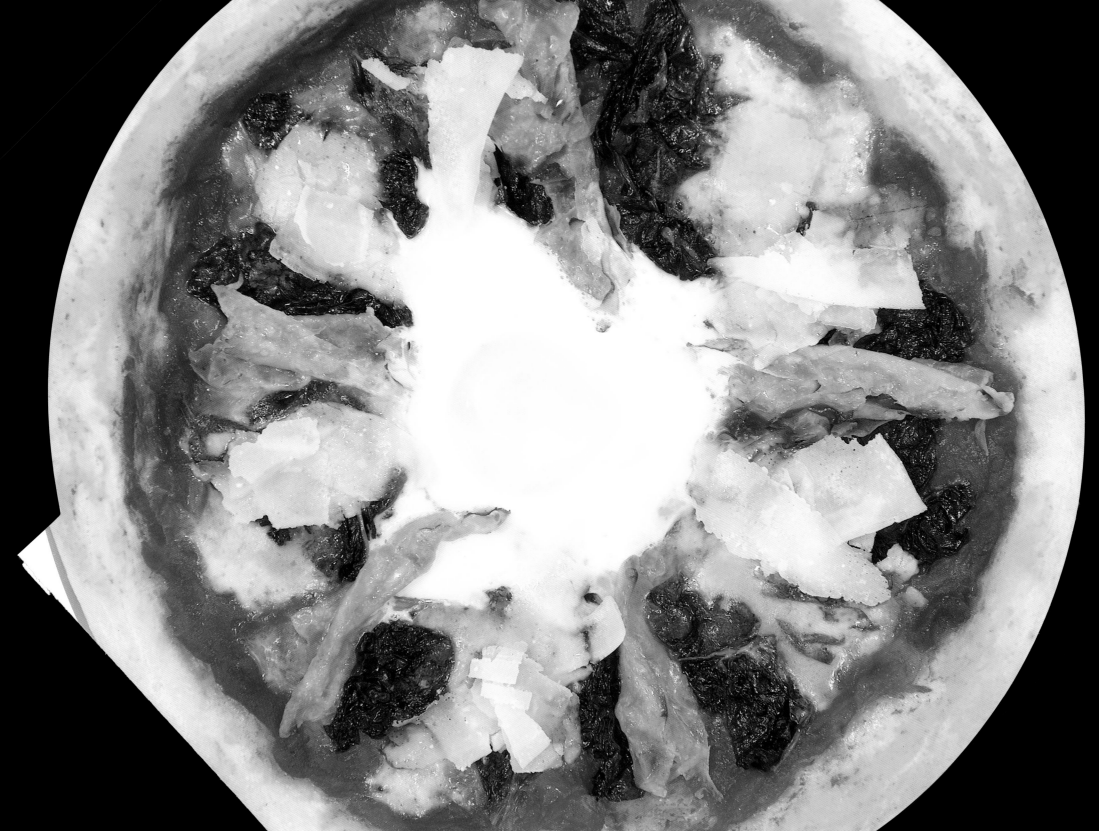

pizza
with **mussels**

CRUST

Basic pizza dough (see pages 8–11)

TOPPING

10–15 mussels, in shell · 1 cup (250 g) diced canned tomatoes, with juice
1 tablespoon finely chopped fresh parsley · 3 cloves garlic, finely chopped
2 tablespoons extra-virgin olive oil · Salt and freshly ground black pepper

SERVES 2 · **PREPARATION** 15 MINUTES + TIME TO SOAK THE MUSSELS, PREPARE THE DOUGH & LET RISE
COOKING 15–25 MINUTES

CRUST **1. Prepare** the pizza dough following the instructions on pages 8–11. Set aside to rise. TOPPING **2. Soak** the mussels in a large bowl of water for 1 hour. **3. Rinse** the mussels in a frying pan over high heat. Stir frequently. They will open after a few minutes. Discard the shells of all but 4 or 5 mussels. Strain the liquid the mussels produce and set aside with the mussels (shelled and in shell) in a bowl. **4. Preheat** the

oven to 500°F (250°C/gas 10). **5. Oil** a 12-inch (30-cm) pizza pan. **6. Knead** the risen pizza dough briefly on a lightly floured work surface, then press it into the prepared pan using your hands. Spread the dough evenly with the tomatoes, leaving a ½-inch (1-cm) border all around. Top with the mussels and sprinkle with the parsley and garlic. Drizzle with the oil. Season with salt and pepper. **8. Bake** for 10–15 minutes, until the crust is crisp and golden brown. **9. Serve** hot.

● **If you liked this recipe, try the Mediterranean pizza on page 94.**

seafood pizza

CRUST

Basic pizza dough (see pages 8–11)

TOPPING

3 tablespoons extra-virgin olive oil · 6 cloves garlic, finely chopped
12 ounces (350 g) mixed fresh or frozen seafood, thawed if frozen · Salt
1½ cups (375 g) diced canned tomatoes, with juice · Freshly ground black pepper

SERVES 2 · PREPARATION 20 MINUTES + TIME TO PREPARE THE DOUGH & LET RISE

COOKING 15–20 MINUTES

CRUST **1. Prepare** the pizza dough following the instructions on pages 8–11. Set aside to rise. **2. Preheat** the oven to 500°F (250°C/gas 10). **3. Oil** a 12-inch (30-cm) pizza pan. TOPPING **4. Heat** 2 tablespoons of oil in a large frying pan over medium heat and sauté half the garlic until pale gold, 2–3 minutes. Add the seafood and sauté over high heat until just tender, 3–5 minutes. Set aside. **5. Knead** the risen pizza dough briefly on a lightly floured work surface, then press it into the prepared pan using your hands. **6. Spread** the dough evenly with the tomatoes and sprinkle with the remaining garlic, leaving a ½-inch (1-cm) border all around. Top with the seafood mixture and drizzle with the remaining 1 tablespoon of oil. Season with salt and pepper. **7. Bake** for 10–15 minutes, until the crust is crisp and golden brown. **8. Serve** hot.

Use any mixture of quick-cooking seafood for this topping: mussels, small shrimp (prawns), baby octopuses, calamari, and fish fillets are all good.

● If you liked this recipe, try the pizza with mussels on page 120.

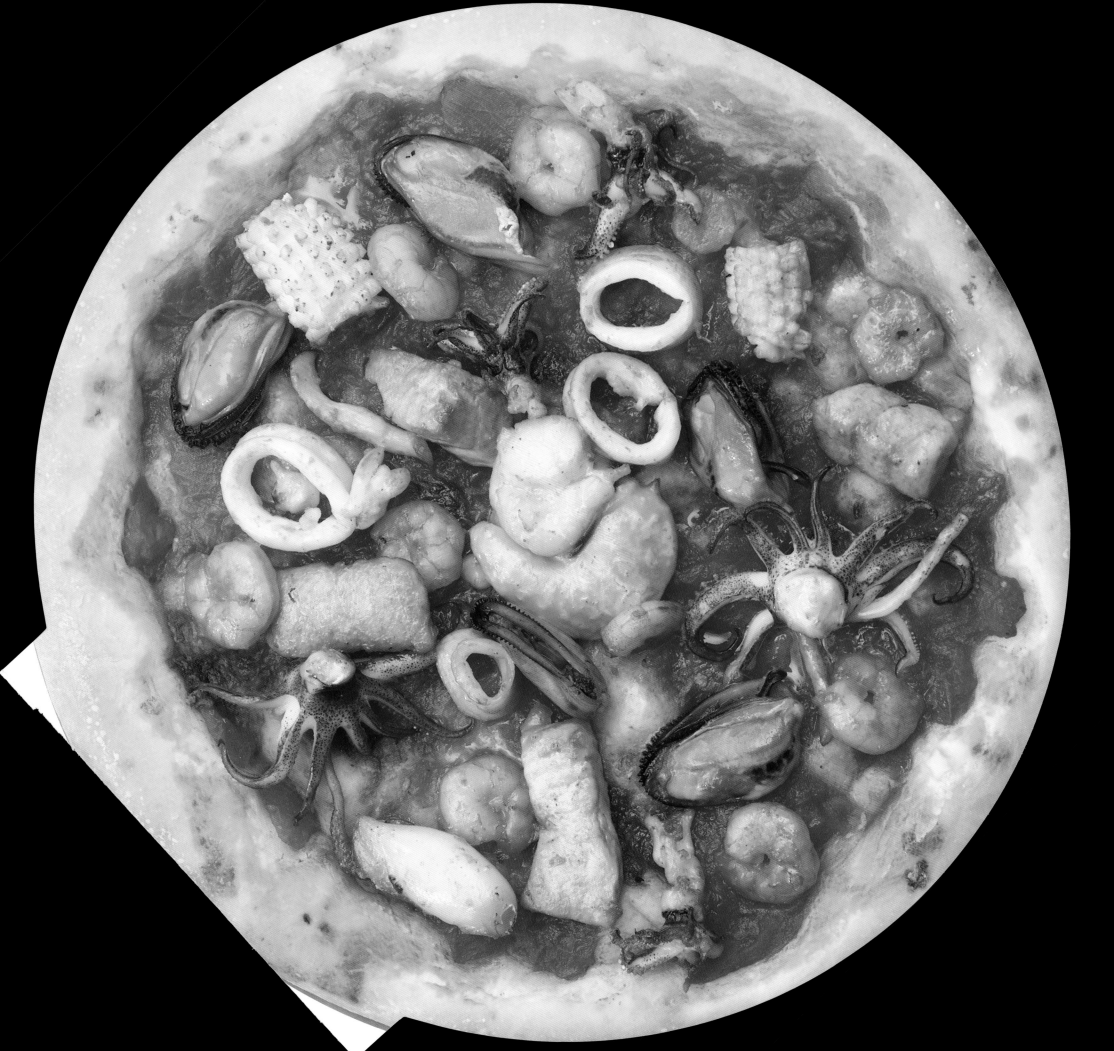

filled pizza with mozzarella, egg & tomatoes

SERVES 2 · PREPARATION 15 MINUTES + TIME TO PREPARE THE DOUGH & LET RISE

COOKING 20–30 MINUTES

CRUST

2 batches basic pizza dough (see pages 8–11)

1 cup (200 g) mashed potatoes

TOPPING

5 ounces (150 g) mozzarella cheese, thinly sliced or shredded · 4–6 leaves fresh basil · 2 hard-boiled eggs, sliced · 4–6 cherry tomatoes, sliced · Salt and freshly ground black pepper · 1 tablespoon extra-virgin olive oil

CRUST **1. Prepare** the pizza dough following the instructions on pages 8–11, incorporating the mashed potatoes into the mixture as you knead. Set aside to rise. **2. Oil** a 12-inch (30-cm) pizza pan. **3. Knead** the risen pizza dough briefly on a lightly floured work surface. Divide the dough in two and press one piece into the prepared pan using your hands.

TOPPING **4. Cover** with the mozzarella, eggs, tomatoes, and basil. Season with salt and pepper and drizzle with the oil. Roll out the remaining dough and cover the filling with it. Pinch around the edges to seal. **5. Cover** with a clean kitchen towel and let rise for 30 minutes. **6. Preheat** the oven to 400°F (200°C/gas 8). **7. Bake** for 20–30 minutes, until risen and golden brown. **8. Serve** hot.

You will need two batches of the medium crust dough (see page 8) to make this pizza.

●If you liked this recipe, try the Calabrian pizza with ricotta & sausage on page 98.

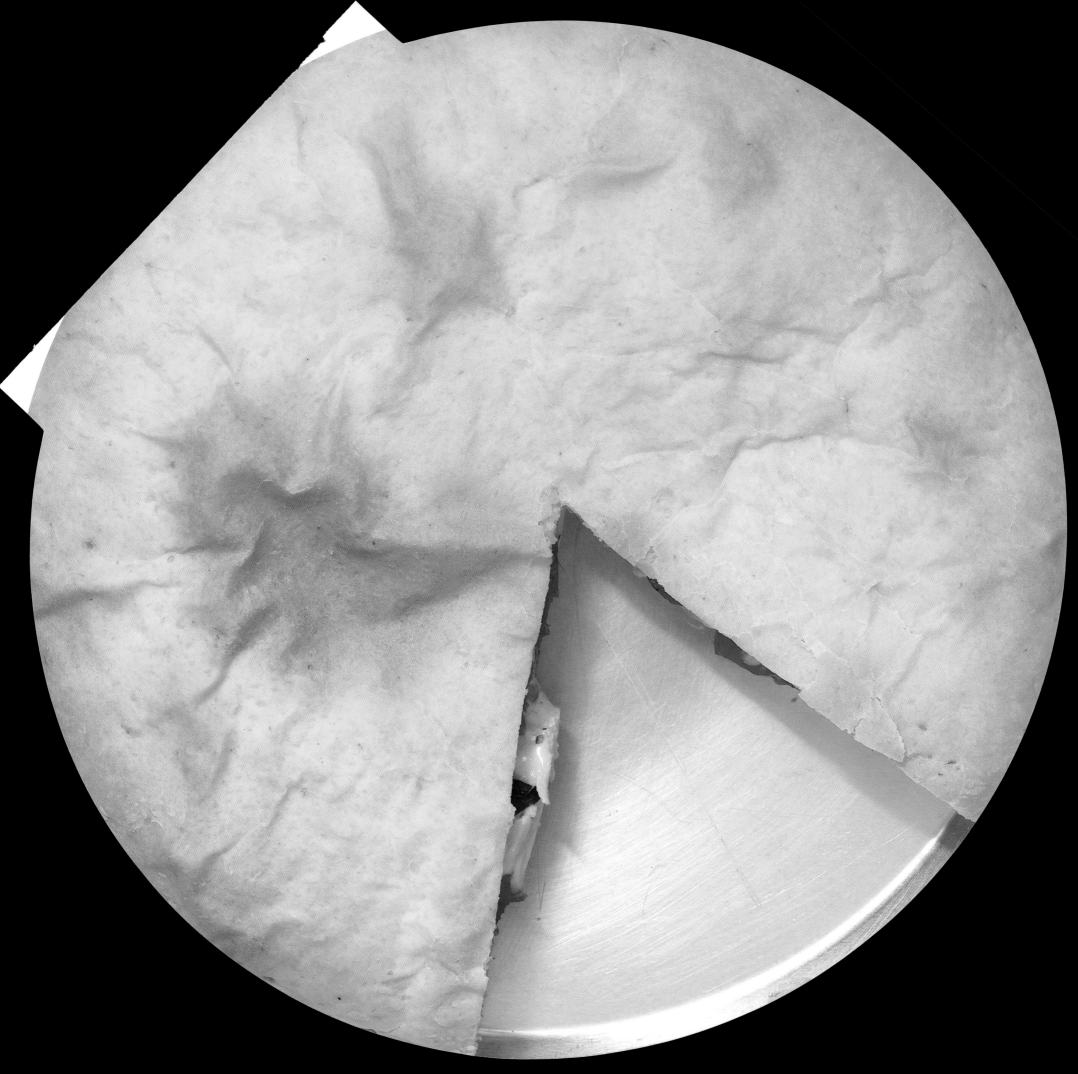

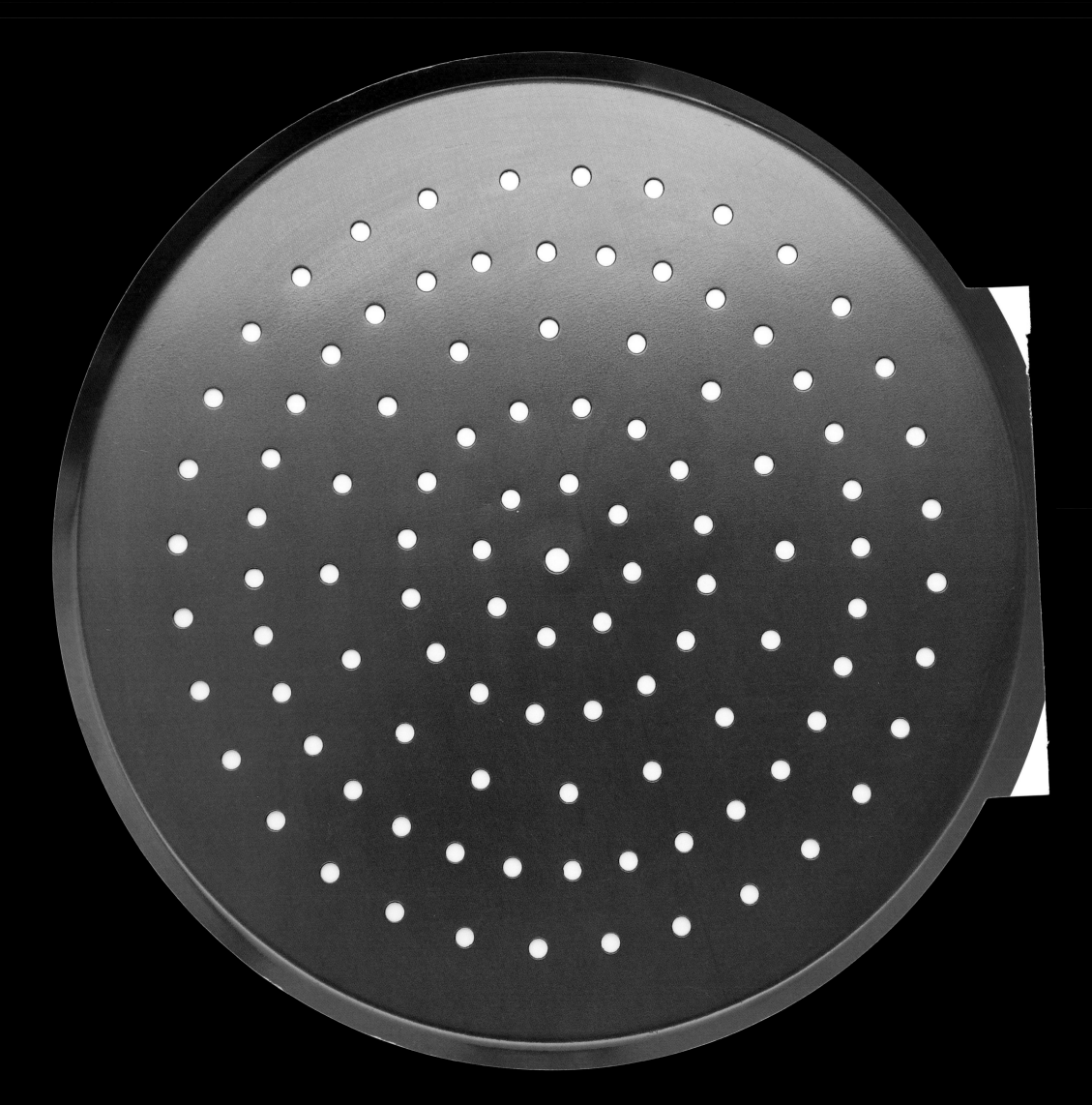

index

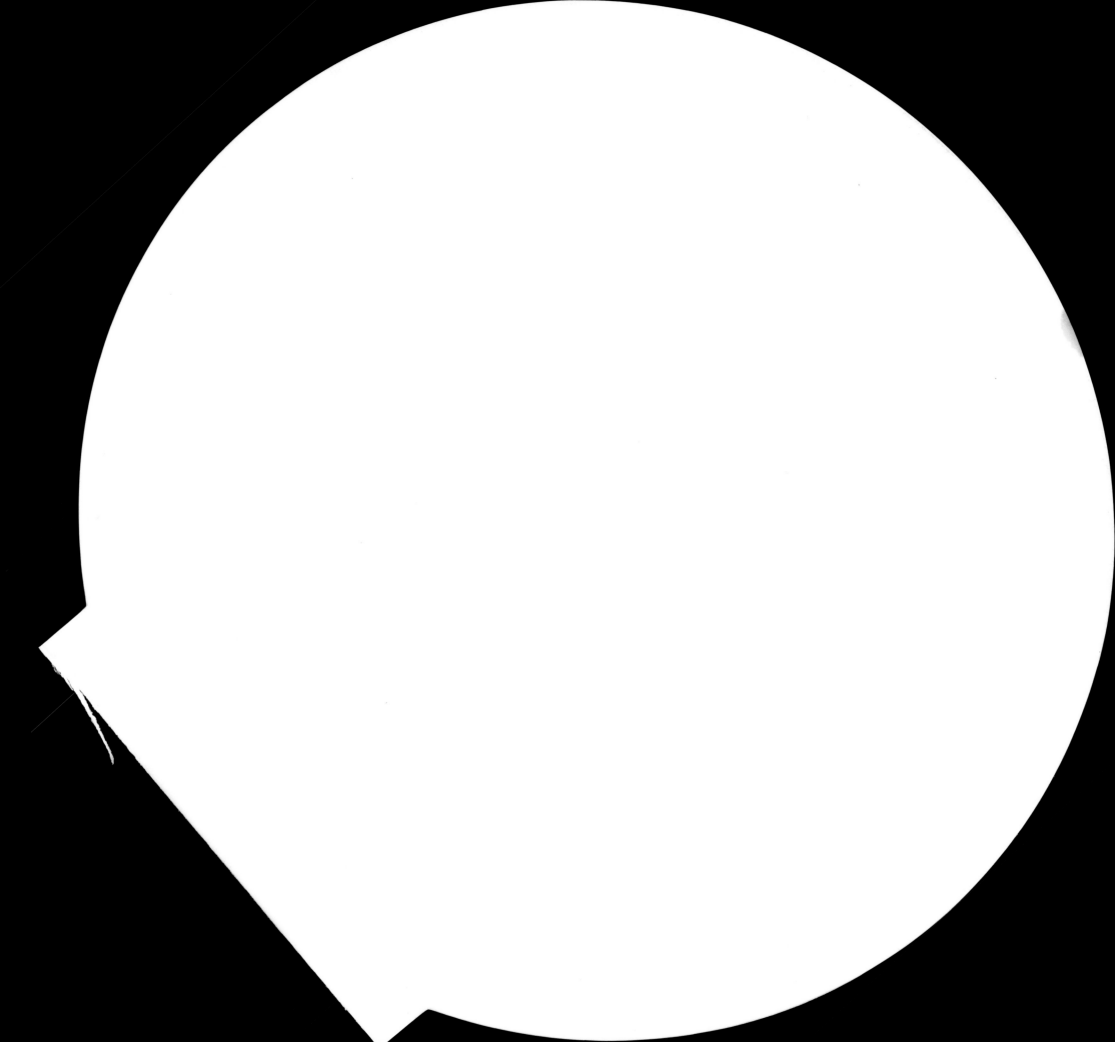

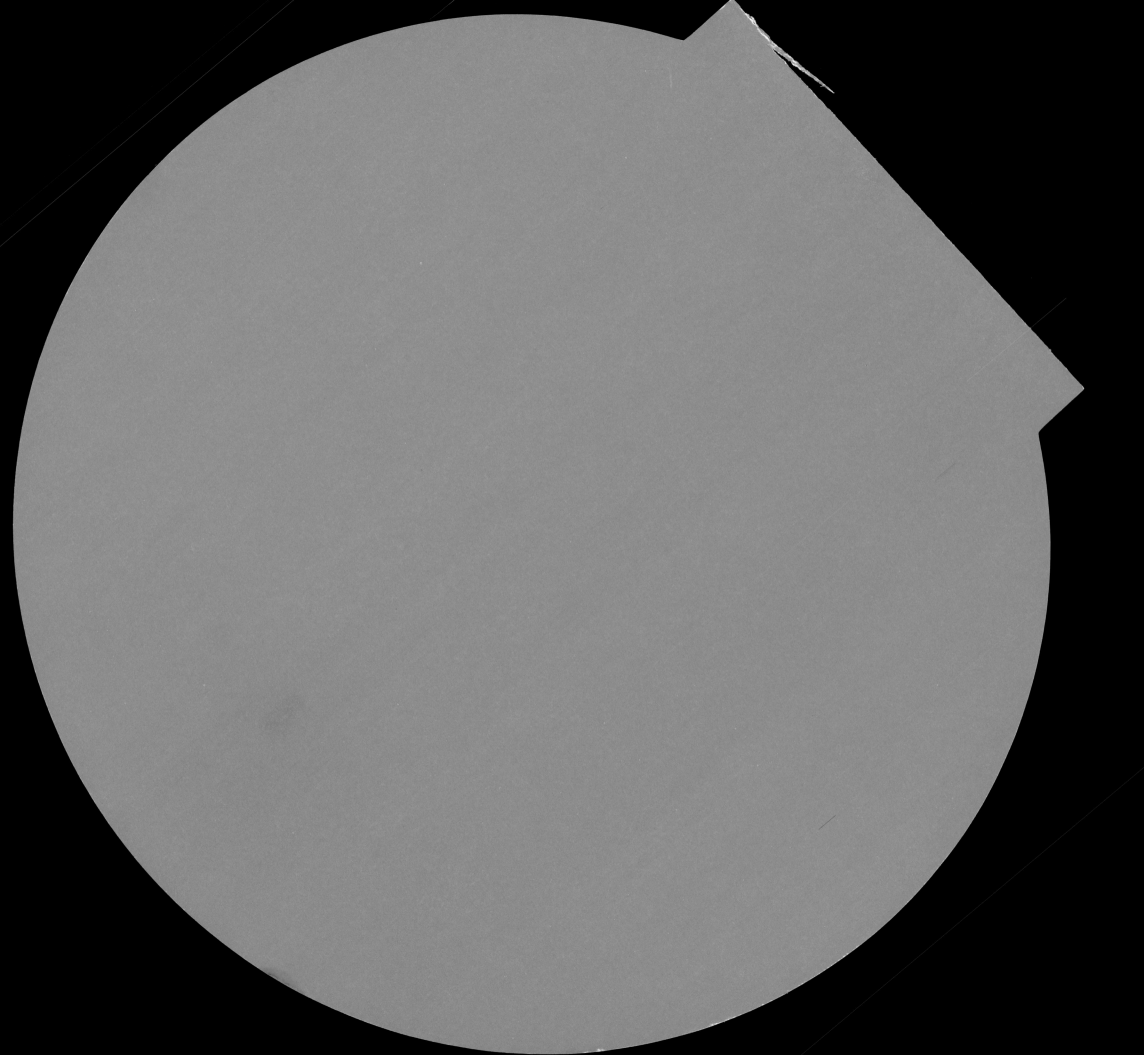